U.S. Aircraft Carriers
in action Part 1

By Robert Stern
Color by Don Greer
Illustrated by Joe Sewell

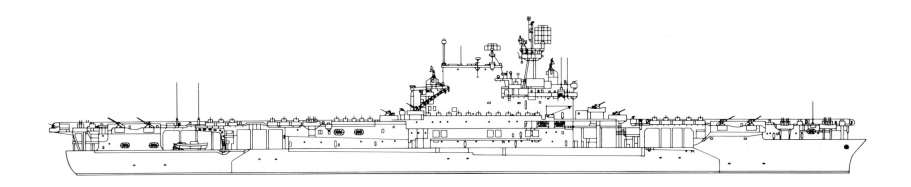

Warships Number 5
squadron/signal publications

A Douglas TBD is launched from USS HORNET (CV8) while enroute to the Battle of Midway. HORNET was later lost during the battle of Santa Cruz.

ISBN 0-89747-265-9

If you have any photographs of the aircraft, armor, soldiers or ships of any nation, particularly wartime snapshots, why not share them with us and help make Squadron/Signal's books all the more interesting and complete in the future. Any photograph sent to us will be copied and the original returned. The donor will be fully credited for any photos used. Please send them to:

Squadron/Signal Publications, Inc.
1115 Crowley Drive.
Carrollton, TX 75011-5010.

Acknowledgements:

The photographs used in this book are all either official U.S. Navy or USAF photos. The Air Force photos came from the Smithsonian National Air and Space Museum collection. I thank Dana Bell for his help in tracking down these photos. The U.S. Navy photos came from either the National Archives & Records Administration (NARA) or the photographic collection of the Naval Historical Center (NHC). The latter collection is under the able administration of Chuck Haberlein.

USS ENTERPRISE (CV-6) (foreground) and the new ESSEX Class carrier USS LEXINGTON (CV-16) (background) launch aircraft while steaming in the Pacific during July of 1944. (NARA)

Introduction

The U.S. Navy had shown considerable interest in aviation as it emerged as a reliable technology at the end of the first and the beginning of the second decade of this century. But, in the U.S. Navy, as in other navies interested in aviation, there was a great deal of controversy over the best way to employ this new capability. There was disagreement even as to whether naval aviation should be considered an independent weapon, or simply an adjunct to the scouting forces in support of the battle line. The general success of aircraft in the land battles of the First World War very quickly led some Navy officials to push for experiments with combat aircraft at sea. Float planes were available, but these were too restricted by weather and sea conditions and were too encumbered by their floats to make effective combat aircraft. Shore-based naval aircraft were indistinguishable from their land-based counterparts, but they were too restricted in range to be an effective weapon over large areas of open water. Both the U.S. and British Royal Navy saw that the potential of this new weapon would be exploited only if the aircraft could be launched from and recovered on ships at sea.

The Royal Navy was the first to build one of this new breed of ship that would carry aircraft to sea. HMS FURIOUS had been launched as a light battlecruiser but was never completed as such. (Her two older sisters, COURAGEOUS and GLORIOUS were both later converted to aircraft carriers, similar to FURIOUS). She was converted prior to completion into a hybrid cruiser/aircraft carrier with a flight deck built up forward of her bridge. This stage of her conversion was completed during July of 1917. This configuration obviously provided the ability to launch aircraft off the bow, but made no provision for their recovery. It was proposed to attempt the recovery of aircraft by sided-slipping around the bridge structure while the ship steamed into the wind at high speed. This was tried only twice and on the second attempt the unfortunate pilot was killed and further attempts were forbidden.

Instead, the Royal Navy opted to modify FURIOUS with a large flying on deck aft of the funnel. This was completed in March of 1918. Narrow ramps on either side of the funnel and bridge allowed aircraft to be moved between the forward and aft flight decks. In this configuration, FURIOUS carried out the first naval air strike against the Zeppelin hangars at Tondern. This pattern of flying on and flying off decks separated by a central superstructure proved dangerous, as well as inconvenient. Turbulence created by the superstructure, as well as hot gasses from the funnel, made recovery a dangerous exercise. The obvious solution was to delete the central superstructure and give FURIOUS a continuous flight deck. During 1922, she returned to the yard for yet another conversion.

The U.S. Navy was forced to follow suit. The theories of ADM Alfred Mahan, taken as gospel in the Navy of that time, stated that commercial rivalry led inevitably to naval conflict. By that standard, the British represented the major post-war threat to the US (of course, this thesis was offset by the sentiment of most officers that the two "Anglo-Saxon" powers would never go to war). To most officers in the U.S. Navy, the most likely enemy in the next war would be Japan, not Great Britain.

The U.S. had led early in the field of naval aviation, but had gotten seriously sidetracked during WWI into a reliance on float planes. At the end of the war, the U.S. found itself seriously behind the British. The Royal Navy had HMS FURIOUS and two other conversions nearing completion (ARGUS and EAGLE) and a purpose-built aircraft carrier under construction (HERMES). The General Board of the Navy met during early 1919, and recommended (in April) the conversion of the new collier USS JUPITER into a flush-decked aircraft carrier. On 20 March 1922, the first American aircraft carrier was commissioned as USS LANGLEY (CV-1). LANGLEY would remain with the fleet until 1936 when she was rebuilt as a seaplane carrier. Her slow speed (14 knots) and small size (13,000 tons) had left her incapable of handling the new generation of faster and heavier monoplanes under development (the Douglas TBD Devastator was accepted by the Navy during January of 1936). During the intervening years she served as the primary test bed for the tactics and technologies that led to the successful deployment of the massive fast carrier task forces that swept the Pacific during the Second World War.

For the first six years of LANGLEY's career, she was the only aircraft carrier in the U.S. Navy. It was 1928 before the next two carriers joined the fleet. Unlike LANGLEY, which was small and slow, these ships, LEXINGTON and SARATOGA, were the largest and fastest aircraft carriers in the world when they were commissioned and were not surpassed in size until IJN SHINANO entered service briefly during 1944. They had been originally laid down as two battlecruisers in a class of six designed to give the U.S. Navy parity with the British and Japanese fleets (HMS HOOD and the IJN AMAGI class battlecruisers were rough contemporaries).

All three major naval powers were planning massive build-ups in their battle fleets immediately following the end of WWI. The Royal Navy, probably better off than the other two in terms of modern capital ships, nevertheless obtained authorization from Parliament during 1921 to begin work on a class of four new battlecruisers and was working up a request for a class of four battleships. The Japanese had their 8-8 Plan of 1916 that called for eight fast new battlecruisers and eight battleships. The U.S., which had continued building ships at a steady pace throughout WWI, commissioning no fewer than four new battleships in the months following the end of the war, had four more battleships nearing completion and had laid down four more battleships and six battlecruisers during 1920-21.

The U.S. Navy based their war plans on the idea that Japan would be the most likely enemy. The annual Fleet Problems, beginning during 1923, were usually based on these plans. After completing Fleet Problem XV, held in 1934, the three aircraft carriers in service (from bottom: LANGLEY, SARATOGA and LEXINGTON) joined the assembled fleet at Colon, Panama. (NARA)

This massive arm build-up on the part of the world's major industrial nations came at a time of popular revulsion in the bloodiness of the recent war and with general public opinion agreeing that a naval arms race between Germany and Britain prior to 1914 had been, at least, a partial cause of that war. Well-meaning legislators in the U.S. Congress, led by SEN Borah, proposed a conference to limit the size of major navies. Amazingly, Britain agreed and was able to pressure the Japanese into playing along. The conference was convened in Washington and, even more amazingly, led to an agreement that limited the capital ship tonnage in the U.S., British and Japanese navies to a proportion of 5:5:3 (France and Italy were dragged along and cajoled into accepting even smaller proportions than the Japanese).

A "Battleship holiday" was declared, meaning that no nation could lay down a new capital ship before 1932. All ships under construction were to be scrapped. Almost as an afterthought, the same proportions were applied to aircraft carrier tonnage, with the British and Americans allowed 135,000 tons each and the Japanese 81,000. LANGLEY and any carrier being built or already in the water was classified as experimental and did not count against these totals. No carrier was to be heavier than 27,000 tons, with the exception of carriers built on existing or under construction capital ship hulls. These could be up to 33,000 tons and could have an additional 3,000 tons of bulges, blisters or deck armor. Each nation could convert two capital ships in this manner.

Under the terms of the Washington Treaty, work was stopped on all six LEXINGTON class battlecruisers during February of 1922. The two, which were most nearly complete, LEXINGTON (CC-1) and SARATOGA (CC-3), were selected for conversion to aircraft carriers and work commenced in July of that year. Work was supposed to be completed in two and a half years, but the ships actually took more than twice as long. It was not until 1928 that the two LEXINGTON class carriers joined the fleet. In the meanwhile, discussions had begun on how to use the 69,000 tons still allowed under the terms of the treaty. Lacking practical experience except with the small and slow LANGLEY, arguments were fought out on the wargaming tables at the Naval War College.

These wargames showed repeatedly that air superiority was a prerequisite for naval victory and that it was won by the side that could get the most aircraft in the air in the critical first few minutes of an engagement. Given the relatively slow pace of flight deck operations

The initial landing trials of the new deck were carried out during March of 1918. The set of longitudinal wires stretched above the deck were supposed to catch the skid rails of the Sopwith Pup fighter and keep it from swerving off the deck while the aircraft skidded to a halt. These early fighters lacked wheel landing gear. (USAF)

This Sopwith Pup missed the wires and engaged a rope barrier strung across the deck to keep the Pup from crashing into the ship's mainmast. Barrier crashes were embarrassing and could result in damage to both pilot and aircraft. (USAF)

The first dedicated aircraft carrier in the world was the Royal Navy's HMS FURIOUS. FURIOUS was launched during 1916 with a flying off deck forward, which displaced one of her two gun turrets. She retained her aft gun turret. (USAF)

at the time and the relatively large amount of space each aircraft was thought to require on the flight deck, it was obvious that more aircraft could only be gained by having more flight decks. This argued strongly for a plan to build five small (13,800 ton) carriers with the remaining tonnage. Proponents of the other mathematical options (four carriers of 17,250 tons, three of 23,000 tons or two of 34,500 tons) argued heatedly that carriers needed greater speed, endurance, armament and protection than could possibly be provided on 13,800 tons. But with absolutely no operational experience to rely on, the decision had to be made based on theory alone (even the U.S. Navy's nominal ally, the Royal Navy, had cut off the flow of data on their much more extensive carrier experience soon after WW I).

Proponents of larger and faster designs argued that aircraft carriers would likely operate far in advance of the battle fleet, putting them at risk of chance encounters with enemy scouting forces. Carriers used in that fashion would need speed to outrun such forces or, if necessary, the strength and durability to slug it out with such forces until help arrived. Supporters of the smaller design argued that carriers would likely be operated near the battleline and would need minimal armor and armament and only enough speed to maneuver easily around 21 knot battleships. The arguments for more, smaller carriers won out and the 13,800 ton, 29 knot RANGER (CV-4) was authorized by Congress during 1930.

Once the issue of RANGER's size had been decided, one more area of contention needed to be resolved: should she be flush-decked or be built with an island structure. Aviators generally wanted a flush deck because it gave them unobstructed flight deck area on which to operate, while ship handlers favored an island because it gave them elevated positions for navigation and gun ranging, but there were other issues as well. LANGLEY had been completed with a flush deck, but the LEXINGTON class had been designed from the start with a massive island structure due to the vastly greater volume of boiler gasses that would have to be vented. LANGLEY had one (later two) hinged funnels,

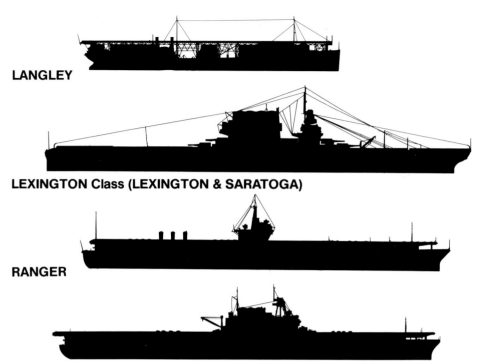

LANGLEY

LEXINGTON Class (LEXINGTON & SARATOGA)

RANGER

YORKTOWN Class (YORKTOWN, ENTERPRISE & HORNET)

WASP

Early in her career, USS LANGLEY had a large pigeon coop under the flight deck round down. The coop held homing pigeons to carry messages. The pigeon coop was deleted soon after her launch. The two stacks folded down during flight operations. (NARA)

The small boat booms were deployed while USS LEXINGTON was at anchor during 1928. The ship's clean hull was a holdover from its battlecruiser design, which caused space in the hangar deck to be limited. The ship was armed with twin 8 inch gun turrets mounted forward and aft of the island. (USAF)

but at 7,150 shaft horse power (shp) she produced trivial amounts of stack gasses compared to the LEXINGTON class' 180,000 shp power plants. RANGER, with a designed shp of 53,500, was going to be a problem if she was built with a flush deck.

Various experiments were tried in the U.S. and elsewhere to eliminate or disperse stack gasses without requiring standard funnels. LANGLEY tried a water spray system to cool the gasses before they came out of the funnels. This caused the gasses to sink towards the water, but in the event, this experiment, along with all the other experiments, proved to be a total failure. RANGER ended up with six, small folding funnels, three on each side, a solution that proved far from ideal. Ironically, RANGER was then completed with an island because the aviators abruptly changed their minds. Even as RANGER was being built, BuAer went back before the General Board and argued strongly for the addition of an island. Experience with the LEXINGTON class, now with the fleet, had shown that an elevated air control position (known in Navy parlance as "pri-fly") was needed to adequately control the flight deck.

When LANGLEY had steadily increased her air complement from eight to twenty and eventually to more than thirty aircraft, her flight deck level air control position had proven inadequate to keep all aircraft in sight. The LEXINGTON class had a pri-fly position built well up on the forward face of their huge funnels and had no similar troubles. A small island structure was added to RANGER while she was being built but it was too late to change the awkward funnel arrangements. All subsequent U.S. carriers, until the adoption of nuclear propulsion, were built with a conventional island incorporating funnels.

Finally, with RANGER nearing completion, Navy attention turned to planning her successors. Enough practical experience had been accumulated with the LEXINGTON class to influence the design process. In the Fleet Exercises of January 1929, the first in which the new carriers had participated, SARATOGA had used her 35 knot speed to perform a night maneuver around the Blue Forces protecting the Panama Canal (forces which included LEXINGTON). She then launched a full deckload for a dawn raid that, in simulation, completely destroyed the canal. The case for larger and faster aircraft carriers was made rather effectively. Further experience was to show that the LEXINGTON class could continue to operate aircraft in far rougher weather than the smaller LANGLEY or RANGER. When the war came in 1941, RANGER was already considered too small and slow for the kind of operations anticipated in the Pacific. Her small size left her unable to mount the number of Anti-Aircraft (AA) batteries considered mandatory for survival in the Pacific, and her complete lack of armor and inadequate internal subdivision made her too vulnerable for that theater. She remained in the Atlantic throughout the war, the only full-size U.S. aircraft carrier to do so.

During 1933, the U.S. Navy again asked Congress for new aircraft carriers. Rather than proceeding with four more RANGER-type ships, the remaining treaty tonnage was to be split between two carriers of approximately 20,000 tons and a third of approximately RANGER's size but built to an improved design. These were to become USS YORKTOWN (CV-5), USS ENTERPRISE (CV-6) and USS WASP (CV-7). The U.S. Navy was a benefactor of the Great Depression that gripped the world's economies beginning in late 1929. Franklin Roosevelt was elected President in 1932 on a platform that included major government spending to put people back to work.

USS RANGER rests at anchor on 11 August 1934; she is largely unchanged since her launch. Her most distinguishing characteristic was the arrangement of six folding funnels, three on each side, aft of her small tower bridge. (NARA)

FDR understood the threat implicit in the continuing expansion of the Imperial Japanese Navy. He was able to address both the public need for work and concerns over Japanese expansion by advocating a massive naval construction program. YORKTOWN and ENTERPRISE were authorized during 1933, WASP in 1935. The Washington Treaty finally lapsed during 1938, with two immediate consequences. The design process began on an improved YORKTOWN, now freed from treaty restrictions. The resulting ESSEX class carriers had a standard displacement of 27,100 tons. USS ESSEX (CV-9) was ordered during 1940. As an interim measure, a third YORKTOWN class carrier was ordered during 1938. USS HORNET (CV-8) was the last U.S. carrier to be completed in time to be available when war in the Pacific broke out. These eight carriers (actually seven because LANGLEY was no longer a carrier) carried the brunt of the battle in the crucial early days of World War II.

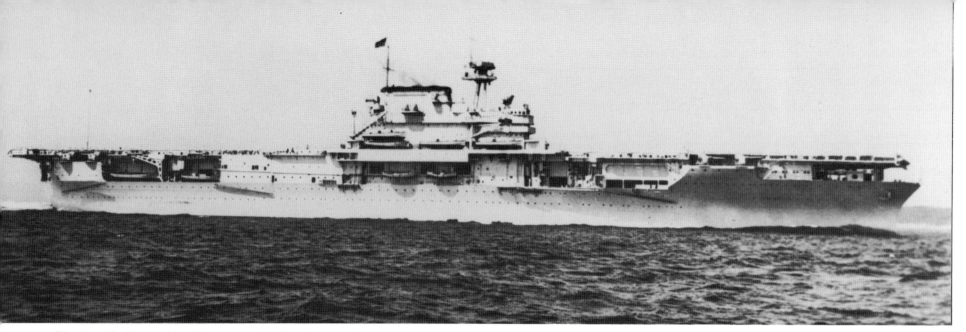

Were it not for the considerably more massive island structure incorporating the funnel, the YORKTOWN class would be hard to distinguish from USS RANGER. The YORKTOWN class was basically an enlarged version of the RANGER. (USAF)

USS WASP was the last of the treaty carriers and her size was greatly restricted due to the remaining tonnage allowed under the terms of the Washington Treaty. WASP had a short career, being lost on 15 September 1942.

Flight Decks

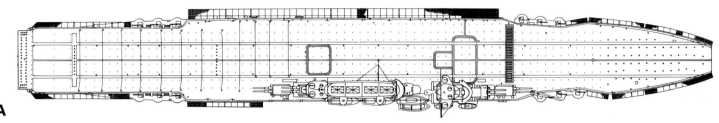

USS SARATOGA

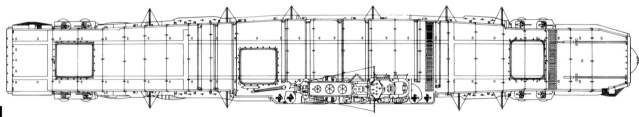

USS YORKTOWN

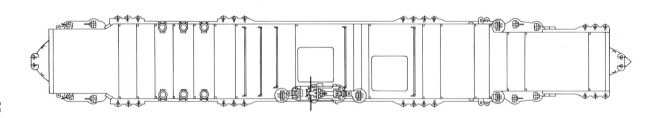

USS RANGER

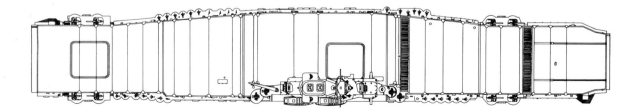

USS WASP

USS LANGLEY
(CV 1, Later AV 3)

The first American aircraft carrier, USS LANGLEY, actually started her career as a collier (USS JUPITER AC 3), before her conversion to a flush deck aircraft carrier during 1922. She was small and slow but had plenty of room and a turbo-electric drive which allowed her to steam astern as fast as ahead. This was considered a useful, possibly even essential, quality in an aircraft carrier, since this would allow aircraft to be recovered over the bow or launched astern. (It was thought that this would become critical if part of the flight deck were damaged: an aircraft carrier that could launch and recover off either end could, in theory, operate with half a flight deck). LANGLEY was completed with no hangar deck, per se; the flight deck was built onto an open trusswork that left the original upper deck of the collier available for aircraft maintenance. (Unlike the British, the U.S. Navy never saw the hangar deck as stowage for combat-ready aircraft. At least through the end of the Second World War, it was normal practice for an American aircraft carrier to keep most, if not all, of her air group on deck when in combat).

During her career as an aircraft carrier, LANGLEY was modified surprisingly little. She was completed with a pair of experimental compressed air catapults, positioned fore and aft, which were removed during 1928. She was armed with four 5"/21 Anti-Aircraft (AA) guns at the hangar deck level, one on each bow and quarter. These were never updated and no other armament was ever added to LANGLEY. As built, she had a single, aft-folding funnel. This was replaced almost immediately by a pair of small, outward-folding funnels. Early on, she was fitted with a large pigeon coop for carrying homing pigeons. The Navy obviously had some nagging doubts about naval aviation, and was literally unwilling to place all of its eggs in one basket. LANGLEY was fitted with fore and aft guide wires, as the British had tried out on FURIOUS, although the set-up on LANGLEY was augmented by transverse arrestor cables. The fear was that an aircraft would veer after landing and possibly pitch overboard. In actual practice, this proved to be largely unwarranted, especially as effective aircraft brakes were developed during the 1920s. The longitudinal wires were removed in 1929.

USS LANGLEY was converted from the collier USS JUPITER at Portsmouth, Virginia. The ship in front of LANGLEY is another collier. LANGLEY had a similar array of cranes amidship which, when cut down, provided the main bracing for the flight deck. (USAF)

LANGLEY's main offensive weapon was her air group. Originally intended to carry eight aircraft, LANGLEY was eventually to carry as many as forty-two aircraft, although her normal air group was set at thirty aircraft.

By 1937, LANGLEY was considered so sufficiently old and obsolete that she was converted into a seaplane tender. This freed up tonnage under the Washington Treaty enabling USS WASP to be built. (Even though excluded from the treaty limits because of her experimental nature, she was counted against that tonnage after 1934 due to the Vinson-Trammell Act). The forward third of her flight deck was removed to free up deck space for her complement of seaplanes. It was in this configuration that she was lost during early 1942, ferrying Army fighters to Java.

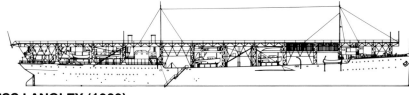

USS LANGLEY (1929)

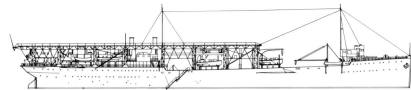

USS LANGLEY (1942)

LANGLEY gets up steam while pier side at Hampton Roads, Virginia during June of 1923. Originally LANGLEY had a single large aft-folding funnel on the port side. This was soon replaced by the twin funnels, which she retained for the remainder of her career. (NARA)

An aircraft tender is tied up alongside USS LANGLEY on 28 April 1925. The open nature of LANGLEY's hangar deck is clearly visible. The twin stacks folded downward into the cutouts visible just below the stack. (USAF)

The same two ships seen from the other side a few days later. The ship had a temporary mast erected in the middle of the flight deck, which was removed when the ship put to sea. The two small masts that appear to be forward on LANGLEY actually belong to the tender. (USAF)

At the end of her career, LANGLEY was converted to a seaplane tender (AV 3) to free up tonnage for new construction under the Washington Treaty. LANGLEY was lost ferrying USAAC P-40s to Java during early 1942. (NHC)

LEXINGTON Class — USS LEXINGTON (CV 2) and USS SARATOGA (CV 3)

The LEXINGTON Class joined the fleet during 1928 and immediately began to prove the case for the large, fast fleet aircraft carrier. Nevertheless, they paid a heavy penalty because their hulls had been originally designed as battlecruisers. The fineness of their hulls gave them a small hangar deck despite their large overall size. (RANGER, on one-third the displacement, had a larger hangar deck). The original hull form was simply extended upward and faired cleanly into the flight deck. This gave them a completely enclosed hangar, a feature unique in American aircraft carrier design and one that would have a role to play in LEXINGTON's loss. It also led to an enclosed weather bow, a feature that would reappear on modern U.S. aircraft carriers.

The LEXINGTON Class retained a reduced version of their original armor layout. They had an armor belt nine and a half feet high varying in thickness from five to seven inches. The original two inch armored deck (thicker over the steering gear) was retained. The flight deck was thin steel plate covered by wood planking. American designers correctly surmised that this construction technique would be easier to repair after damage than an armored flight deck. (The Royal Navy took a completely different tack, opting for an armored flight deck on their purpose-built aircraft carriers. The British have

claimed that flight deck armor saved several of their aircraft carriers during The Second World War. The Americans countered that the penalties paid by the British, including decreased stability in a seaway [due to the weight of armor carried high above the waterline], a shallow hangar [because a deep hangar would only increase the height of the armor above the waterline] and the fact that the flight deck, once damaged, could only be repaired in a shipyard [while the Americans were often able to absorb bomb damage and make the flight deck operable again after only minutes or hours of at sea repairs] were too much and that that they would accept the risk of losing a ship that might have been saved by flight deck armor. In fact, it is impossible to point to a single loss among this set of aircraft carriers that flight deck armor would have prevented). Being so finely faired into the hull, the flight deck of the LEXINGTON Class, as built, tapered sharply at the bow.

The LEXINGTON Class was armed with eight 8 inch guns in four mounts, two fore and two aft of the massive island. Twelve 5"/21 AA guns in open single mounts were positioned in threes on sponsons on each bow and quarter. Both carriers had a single flywheel catapult to launch large seaplanes over the bow. (It was not until late in WWII that naval aircraft became so heavy that a rolling takeoff over the bow, without the benefit of catapult, became impractical). This model was no more successful than LANGLEY's compressed air catapult and was removed from both carriers in about 1934.

The LEXINGTON Class was powered by turbo-electric drive, as was LANGLEY. Their massive power plants, the biggest for any U.S. Navy warship at that time, produced 180,000 shaft horse power, driving them through the water at a top speed of 34 knots.

Neither carrier was extensively modified prior to the outbreak of the war. The closer hostilities came, the more reluctant the Navy was to release either of their biggest carriers for a lengthy refit. Plans were drawn up to add a substantial light AA battery, widen the flight deck forward and add a stability blister on the port side. (Both ships had to leave fuel spaces on the starboard side unfilled, reducing their fuel capacity, to prevent a permanent starboard list due to the weight of their island structure and 8 inch batteries). This work, however, was either indefinitely postponed or carried out piecemeal.

LEXINGTON (1928)

LEXINGTON (1942)

SARATOGA (1943)

The USS LEXINGTON at anchor off Panama on 25 March 1928, was a significant addition to the fleet. The massive funnel, separated from the bridge, was a recognition feature of the LEXINGTON Class carriers. At this point she was armed with four eight inch twin gun mounts. (NHC)

At the outbreak of war, LEXINGTON was the more modernized of the two, having had her flight deck widened forward during 1936, a CXAM-1 radar fitted and a more extensive light and medium AA suite added. For SARATOGA, the planned modifications, with the exception of fitting some light and medium AA guns, had to wait until she was torpedoed in January of 1942. During her repairs at Puget Sound, she received an extensive refit that lasted until May. During that refit, she received a stability blister, had her 8 inch mounts replaced with an equal number of twin 5"/38 gun mounts and had four of the newly licensed Bofors 40MM quad gun mounts installed. At this same time, the three single 5 inch gun mounts on each corner were replaced by a pair of single 5"/38s. LEXINGTON discarded her 8 inch mounts during April of 1942, replacing them with additional 1.1 inch quad gun mounts. She went into the battle of the Coral Sea, where she was sunk, mounting twelve 5"/21s, twelve 1.1 inch quad mounts, thirty-two 20MM and twenty-eight .50 caliber anti-aircraft guns. SARATOGA emerged from her refit with sixteen 5"/38, four 40MM quad mounts, five 1.1 inch quads and thirty 20MM guns. (The experience of the first battles had shown the uselessness of the .50 caliber machine gun as an anti-aircraft weapon). Torpedoed again in August 1942, she emerged from those repairs with 40MM quads replacing her 1.1 inch guns and twenty-two additional 20MM mounts.

SARATOGA was refitted again during late 1943, receiving sixteen more twin and quad 40MM mounts. In mid-1944, as she was working up as a night operations carrier, she received a pair of hydraulic catapults forward. After she was damaged off Iwo Jima during February 1945, she was never fully operational again.

Based on experience with LANGLEY, the LEXINGTON Class was built to handle an air group of ninety aircraft on their massive flight decks. By 1942, their complement was still eighty-eight, although naval aircraft had, in the meanwhile, gotten significantly larger and heavier. By late 1944, SARATOGA, now a night carrier, had an air group of sixty-nine aircraft.

The two sister ships of the LEXINGTON Class, USS LEXINGTON and USS SARATOGA were virtually indistinguishable. SARATOGA rides at anchor with a number of small boats moored aft. The small aft elevator, alongside the aft 8" gun mounts, is open while the outline of the larger forward elevator is visible abreast the bridge. The elevator arrangement proved to be a handicap and all subsequent fleet carriers had at least three. (USAF)

The similarity between the two ships eventually led to the adoption of a broad Black funnel stripe to identify SARATOGA. By this time (12 August 1930), SARATOGA had added a catwalk midway up her funnel, allowing movement between pri-fly on the forward face of the funnel and the aft control station. LEXINGTON had a similar catwalk since 1928. (USAF)

As a further identification aid, the ships had their nicknames (LEX and SARA) painted in large White letters just above the flight deck round down. Later, U.S. aircraft carriers would paint their hull numbers on both ends of the flight deck for this same reason. (NARA)

SARATOGA gets underway from San Diego, California during May of 1932. The Black funnel band and her nickname (SARA) in White on the round down make identification easy. The forward elevator is down. (NARA).

For part of the prewar period, SARATOGA also sported a large White "E" award on the funnel stripe. Generally an "E" award painted on the funnel meant that the award was for excellence in engineering. (NARA)

LEXINGTON was painted in Ms 1 and Ms 5 camouflage before the outbreak of the Second World War. At this time (14 October 1941), she still carried her 8 inch gun mounts, each topped by a pair of .50 caliber machine guns in gun tubs. She has replaced the catwalk on her funnel with a gallery of additional .50 caliber mounts higher up on the funnel. Additionally, the flight deck had been widened near the bow. (NARA)

LEXINGTON is down at the bow due to torpedo damage sustained at the Battle of Coral Sea. She carries galleries for .50 caliber machine guns and single 20MM mounts run along the funnel at two levels and in the boat stowage space aft. Her 8 inch guns were replaced during April of 1942 by 1.1 inch quad anti-aircraft guns. CXAM-1 radar was added on the forward lip of the funnel. (NHC)

5 Inch Dual Mount

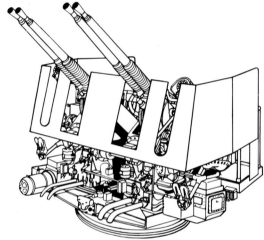

40MM Quad Mount

20MM Single Mount

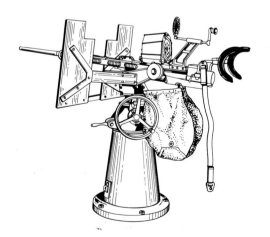

SARATOGA returned to Pearl Harbor following torpedo damage repairs on 6 June 1942. She has had most of the changes that were previously made to LEXINGTON, including the widened bow, CXAM-1 radar and the 20MM gun gallery decks (the .50 caliber guns were deleted because this gun was now accepted as useless for air defense). Additionally, she has had her 8 inch mounts replaced by 5"/38 dual mounts. Her bridge has been cut down and simplified and Mk 37 directors with FD radar have been added to control the 5 inch DP mounts. (NARA)

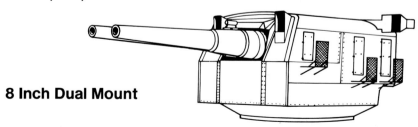

8 Inch Dual Mount

The **SARATOGA** during September of 1942 (above) and June of 1944 (below). The most noticeable change in the ship has been the addition of numerous quad 40mm gun mounts in individual sponsons along the sides. She retained, however, the outdated CXAM-1 radar antenna. (NARA)

SARATOGA emerged from a major refit/overhaul during the Summer of 1944 with a distinctive Measure 32/11A camouflage. She has had her radar suite updated with an SK search radar antenna mounted on her foremast and an SM fighter direction radar antenna replacing the CXAM-1 antenna on her funnel. Additionally, there were qaud 40мм gun sponsons suspended under the flight deck round down. (NARA)

SARATOGA steams at high speed with a battleship escort in the background. The oval objects on her funnel are life rafts. (USN)

The White spots on SARATOGA's bridge on 22 February 1945 were shrapnel damage from a Kamikaze attack on 21 February. The SM radar on its substantial pedestal is mounted at the front edge of the funnel, while the Mk 4/22 radar combination on her bridge was unusual. The Mk 22 "orange peel" antenna was normally teamed with the later Mk 12 radar. (NARA)

Late in her career SARATOGA served as a training aircraft carrier. Her small aft elevator, too small to handle modern aircraft, was deleted and much of her hangar deck given over to classrooms. The aircraft on the bow are Avengers. (NARA)

USS RANGER (CV 4)

Although too small and slow for action in the Pacific, RANGER nevertheless set the pattern followed by later, larger and more successful designs. She was built with a large, open hangar deck high enough to store assembled aircraft in the overhead with sufficient clearance for routine aircraft storage and maintenance below. She had a compact bridge island structure that included a command station, gun control stations and pri-fly (primary air control). Her conventional geared-turbine power plant produced 53,500 shp, which drove the ship at a maximum of 29.5 knots. (Her size was too small to accommodate a turbo-electric power plant, which took up considerably more room than a conventional power plant of similar output. This problem and the greater vulnerability of turbo-electric systems, gradually led to the abandonment of that type of power plant).

The gasses from her boilers were led up to six outward-folding funnels, three on each side aft. She was armed, at the time of her launch, with eight 5"/25 single mounts arranged two in each quadrant on gallery deck sponsons and forty .50 cal machine guns for close-in defense arranged along the flight deck galleries. This extensive gallery deck running the full length of her flight deck was a new feature that became standard on all later designs. The most serious deficiency resulting from her small size and light displacement, more serious even than her relatively slow speed, was her near total lack of armor and torpedo compartmentation.

After a refit during 1941, RANGER mounted six 1.1 inch quad gun mounts replacing sixteen of her .50 cal machine guns. This was upgraded again during mid-1942 to six 40MM quads and thirty 20MM single mounts. This was considered to be an inadequate level of AA armament, but being so small, she had no more reserve stability to allow for additional top weight. By January 1943, she mounted forty-six 20MM mounts, but this left her dangerously unstable and during the Fall, six of these were removed.

There was some discussion of a major refit to make RANGER truly combat-worthy, but this would have taken up yard space and material needed for more important warships and, in the event, was never carried out. Instead, she discarded all eight of her 5 inch guns, received a bow catapult, a full radar suite and was assigned the task of training night fighter units.

Her intended air group was seventy-six aircraft. During 1942, she operated seventy-two FM Wildcats and SBD Dauntless dive bombers.

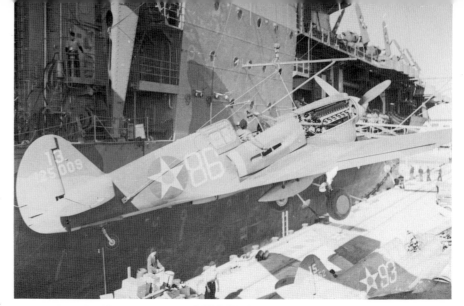

Army Air Force P-40Es are loaded into RANGER's hangar on 15 April 1942. The fighters were to be flown off to Accra, for transit on to India. The aircraft on the bow are SB2Us, part of the RANGER air group.

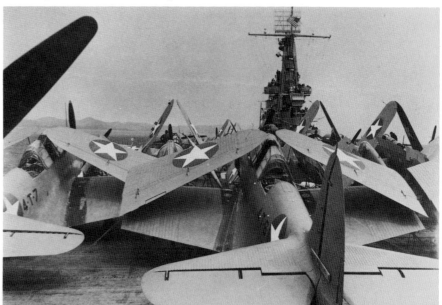

RANGER's air group (CVG4) included (from foreground to background) TBDs, F4Fs and SB2Us, all obsolescent by 18 June 1942. Ranger carried an FD radar (facing aft on the island) and a large CXAM-1 antenna on top of the mainmast.

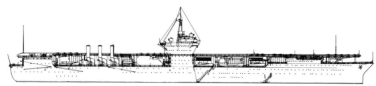

RANGER (1940)

RANGER (1943)

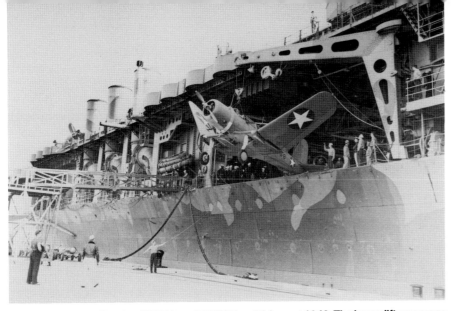

Aircraft handlers offload an SB2U from RANGER on 24 August 1942. The heavy lift crane was used as an aircraft handling crane, as well as for other large, heavy loads such as ammunition. The ship was painted in Measure 12 Mod camouflage.

Serving as a training carrier, RANGER operated FM Wildcats, TBM Avengers and SBD Dauntless dive bombers. The crew is conducting a General Quarters drill with all 5"/25 gun mounts, 40 and 20MM guns manned with the crews in helmets and life jackets. (NARA)

At the time of the Operation TORCH landings, November of 1942, RANGER was carrying CBG41. The air wing had replaced its earlier SB2U dive bombers with Douglas SBDs. The Dauntless all carry the special Yellow surround on the national insignia adopted for Operation TORCH. (NARA)

RANGER rests at anchor off Placentia on 10 April 1943. She is camouflaged in the mid-war Atlantic scheme, Measure 22. This was the camouflage that she carried for most of the war. Her folding funnels are tilted outward and she has 40MM quad gun mounts fore and aft of her island and on either side forward. (NARA)

YORKTOWN Class — USS YORKTOWN (CV 5), USS ENTERPRISE (CV 6) and USS HORNET (CV 8)

The first class of U.S. aircraft carriers designed with the benefit of real operating experience, the YORKTOWN Class carried an air group the size of RANGER's at speed and range closer to LEXINGTON and with some measure of protection for their hulls. The YORKTOWN Class were essentially an enlarged version of RANGER: they shared the basic design principles of a large, open hangar deck topped by a thin, rectangular wood and steel flight deck.

The YORKTOWN Class differed primarily, besides being larger than RANGER, in having their funnels built into the island structure. By the time the YORKTOWN Class was designed, the fascination with turbo-electric drive had finally cooled, and they were planned from the beginning to be powered by standard geared-turbine machinery. Their power plants generated 120,000 shp for a speed of 33 knots. The design of the power plant, however, was flawed by a poor arrangement of components. All three boiler rooms were positioned adjacent to each other, followed by the two engine rooms. This meant that a ship could be immobilized by relatively minor damage, as happened to HORNET at Santa Cruz. Later U.S. designs alternated boiler and engine rooms.

The YORKTOWN Class carried a narrow armor belt of 4 inches tapering to 2.5 inches, triple torpedo bulkheads and hangar deck and main deck armor equivalent to 3 inches of horizontal armor. They were fitted with four catapults, two at the bow and two aimed sideways out of the hangar deck. One of these launched to each side through large openings in the hangar deck forward of the bridge. The idea for hangar deck catapults came from exercises in which full deckloads of strike aircraft had to be launched from LEXINGTON or SARATOGA in order to free the flight deck to send out a small scouting mission. The notion was that scouting missions, which often are required at very short notice, could be launched from the hangar deck without disturbing the deckload of strike aircraft on the flight deck. In practice, the hangar deck catapults were rarely, if ever, used, in part because the role of scout and bomber aircraft were increasingly combined in the same aircraft, culminating in the highly successful SBD Dauntless, allowing the air group far greater flexibility. The hangar deck catapults were removed from ENTERPRISE and HORNET during June of 1942; the flight deck catapults were retained on ENTERPRISE but came into regular use only in 1944.

At launch, the YORKTOWN Class all carried eight 5"/38 in single mounts arranged at the corners as on RANGER. Fire control was provided by a pair of Mk 33 directors mounted on the island. Four 1.1 inch quad mounts were located two each fore and aft of the island and twenty-four .50 cal. machine guns were mounted at the gallery deck level. HORNET differed only in having the later Mk 37 directors installed in place of the Mk 33s. YORKTOWN had twenty-four 20MM single mounts fitted prior to her loss at Midway. HORNET had a similar number and ENTERPRISE mounted thirty-two 20MM at that time.

USS YORKTOWN at anchor at Hampton Roads, Virginia, on 30 October 1937. Like RANGER, she had a large, open hangar deck, equipped with sliding steel shutters that provided weather protection. A gallery deck surrounds the flight deck, even extending under the bow. (NHC)

The two surviving YORKTOWN Class ships both had a fifth 1.1 inch mount added at the bow after Midway. At the time of HORNET's loss, she had her 20MM battery increased to thirty-two and ENTERPRISE had been increased to thirty-eight. ENTERPRISE had her 1.1 inch mounts replaced by 40MM quads soon after Santa Cruz, but since the new mounts were significantly heavier, this led to severe overloading.

A mid-1943 refit for ENTERPRISE included the addition of blisters which served to increase both underwater protection and stability. She now mounted six 40MM quads, eight 40MM twins and forty-eight 20MM single mounts. Her displacement had grown to 32,000 tons. Her air group had grown from ninety aircraft (prewar) to ninety-one during late 1943. She received one final refit after being damaged in 1945. ENTERPRISE then mounted eleven 40MM quads, five 40MM twins and sixteen 20MM twin mounts, but she was never to see combat again.

YORKTOWN received a CXAM radar during 1940, ENTERPRISE a CXAM-1 at about the same time and HORNET was completed mounting an SC air search set. While the SC's electronics were better than either version of the CXAM, its smaller antenna gave it poorer performance, so during mid-1942, HORNET was fitted with a CXAM antenna off a damaged cruiser. ENTERPRISE received an SC-2 radar during late 1942 to supplement her CXAM-1. This was later replaced by an SK in 1943, at which time an SM height finder was also added.

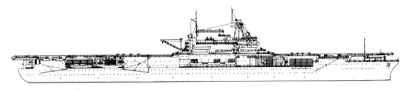

YORKTOWN (1937)

HORNET (1942)

ENTERPRISE (1945)

After ENTERPRISE was launched during 1939, it became critical to be able to distinguish between the nearly identical sisters (much as had been the case with the LEXINGTON Class). To aid in identification YORKTOWN began sporting a large black "Y" painted on her funnel.

23

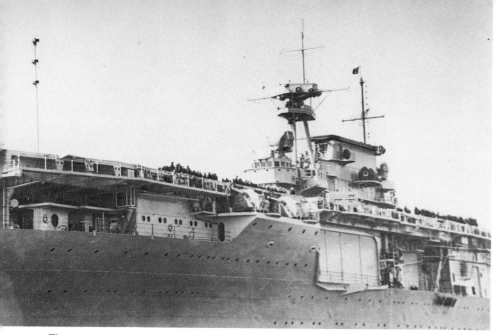

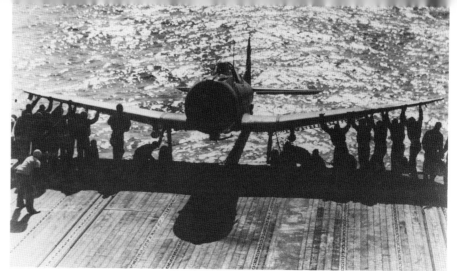

The two covered guns on the sponson just forward of the closed hangar bay are 5 inch anti-aircraft guns. The object projecting from the hangar bay is the end of the forward cross deck hangar catapult. (NHC)

Since it was normal American practice to carry a full air group on deck, finding out of the way places to stow aircraft was critical. One attempt was this outrigger arrangement on ENTERPRISE. The tail wheel of the SBD would be guided into the groove in the outrigger and the aircraft backed up until its main wheels were at the edge of the deck. (NARA)

ENTERPRISE was distinguished by the letters "EN" painted in large White letters on the flight deck. The aircraft on deck are TBDs, F3Fs, SB2Us, and Northrop BTs. (NARA & USAF)

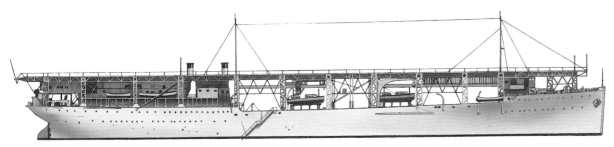

The USS LANGLEY (CV1) was the U.S. Navy's first aircraft carrier, converted from the collier USS JUPITER.

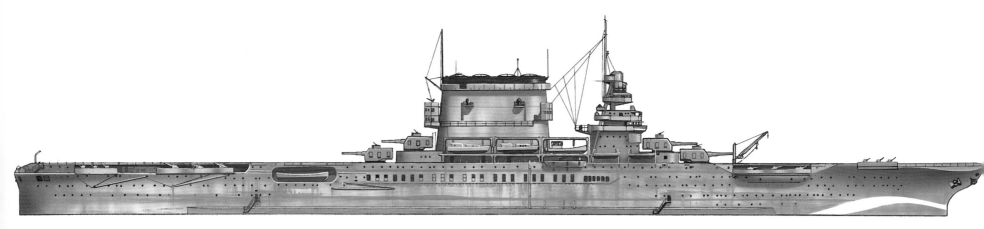

USS LEXINGTON (CV2) carried a camouflage of Measure 1 (Dark Gray) with a White bow wave during late 1939. The false bow wave gave the impression of high speed even when the ship was dead in the water.

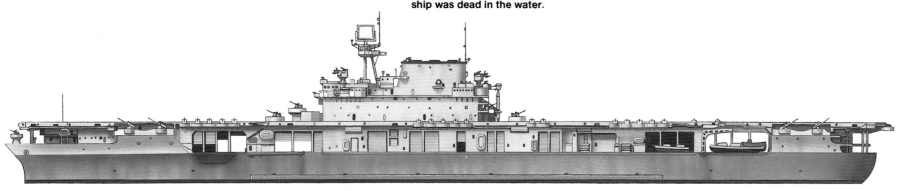

During early 1942, USS YORKTOWN (CV5) was painted in two tone (Sea Blue and Ocean Gray) Measure 12 camouflage used to make identification and ranging difficult for surface and subsurface opponents.

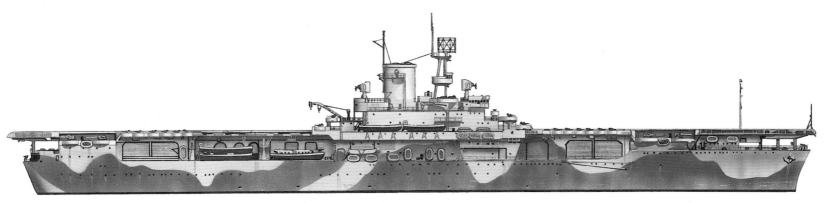

USS WASP (CV7) carried a Measure 12 Modified camouflage. The wave pattern was intended to make accurate speed and range estimates more difficult for enemy ships.

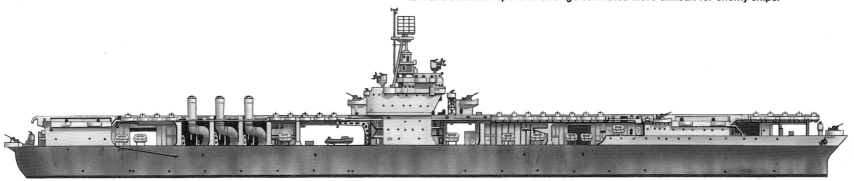

USS RANGER (CV4) carried Measure 22 (Sea Blue and Haze Gray) camouflage during April of 1943. During this period WASP operated with the British Navy in the Atlantic.

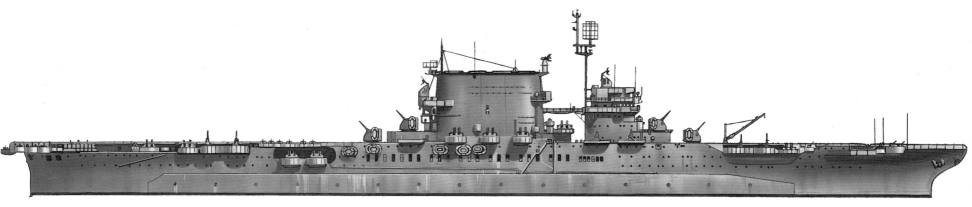

USS SARATOGA (CV3) carried Measure 21 (Navy Blue) camouflage during 1944. Modernized with radar, 5 inch gun turrets and numerous anti-aircraft mounts, she was a far different ship than the SARATOGA of 1939. MS 21 was effective against aerial observers.

YORKTOWN arrives at Pearl Harbor on 27 May 1942. She has a CXAM radar on the foremast and quad 1.1 inch anti-aircraft mounts fore and aft of the island. The AA directors are the lightweight Mk 33s, normally reserved for cruisers. (NHC)

ENTERPRISE is back at Pearl Harbor after her abortive sortie to the South Pacific and just a day before leaving for Midway. She appears to be painted in Measure 11 camouflage, which looks darker due to the overcast skies. Her only radar is a CXAM-1 on her foremast. (NARA)

27

The YORKTOWN rests in dry dock at Pearl Harbor, on 27 May 1942. She suffered considerable structural damage at the Battle of the Coral Sea, and the twenty-four hours she was allowed in dry dock before leaving for Midway was insufficient to repair even the most serious damage. She is painted in standard Measure 12 camouflage. (NARA)

The third YORKTOWN class aircraft carrier was USS HORNET moored at Pearl Harbor about the time of Midway. Being of later construction, there were some minor differences between HORNET and her older sisters. She carried the newer, heavier Mk 37 gun directors on the island and, to compensate, had lighter foretops. She was painted in Measure 12 Mod camouflage. The long gun barrel is a 5"/38 anti-aircraft gun and the gun tubs under the bow are for 20mm guns. HORNET gained fame as the ship that launched the Doolittle raiders against Tokyo. (NARA)

YORKTOWN, with her air group back onboard, about 1400 on 4 June 1942, awaits word on HIRYU's location before launching an attack to finish off the last enemy aircraft carrier remaining afloat at the Battle of Midway.

While waiting to launch her next strike, YORKTOWN was attacked by three Japanese dive bombers, which started minor fires at the base of her funnel and among the parked aircraft on the flight deck. These fires were quickly brought under control.

At 1445 on 4 June, YORKTOWN was hit by two torpedos which led the captain to abandon ship. She survived those two torpedos and was still afloat two days later when, hit by two more torpedos, she was finally sunk. (NARA)

The Battle of Santa Cruz (26 October 1942) was the last major carrier battle in the South Pacific. During the battle, ENTERPRISE survived sustained attacks by Japanese aircraft including this Kate, which turned away after releasing its torpedo.

The torpedo missed ENTERPRISE, as did all others aimed at her in the war, but HORNET was not as lucky. HORNET was hit by a total of three torpedos and five bombs, which was enough to doom her. The destroyer USS RUSSELL (DD 414) stands alongside after the first attack left HORNET without power. (NARA)

ENTERPRISE steams at high speed while engaged in raids against Palau during March of 1944. Numerous 40mm gun mounts have been added, although she was considered too small to carry twin 5" turrets at flight deck level.

31

During 1944, the radar suite on ENTERPRISE included SK and SP antennas on her foremast and an SC-2 antenna on a small outrigger abreast the funnel. The aircraft aft the island are Grumman F6F Hellcats. By this time the Hellcat had taken over as the primary carrier fighter. (NARA)

ENTERPRISE briefly carried Ms 32/4Ab camouflage between July 1944 and January 1945, after which time she reverted to Measure 21 camouflage. This camouflage was painted on during a hasty refit at Puget Sound that ended during early August of 1944.

ENTERPRISE steams off Luzon, the Philippines. The day before, 30 October 1944, she was hit by kamikazes; although damaged she remained in action. A week earlier ENTERPRISE aircraft had been involved in the successful attacks against the Japanese battleship MUSASHI. (NARA)

ENTERPRISE steams into the wind to recover her air group on 13 April 1944. The task force was enroute to Hollandia and included the ESSEX class carrier LEXINGTON (CV16). (NARA)

USS WASP (CV 7)

The last of the treaty carriers, WASP's design was greatly restricted due to the limited tonnage remaining under the limitations of the Washington Treaty. To save weight, a number of clever ideas were tried out. She had an asymmetrical hull, being bulged to the port, in order to counterbalance her island without added ballast. She was also given a T-shaped deck edge elevator in place of a third centerline elevator.

WASP was shorter than RANGER, whom she matched closely in displacement, requiring a larger power plant (70,000 shp) in order to reach her designed speed of 29 knots. There was no room for armor in her design, though she did have far better anti-torpedo subdivision than RANGER.

At launch, she carried eight 5"/38 single mounts, four 1.1 inch quads and twenty-four .50 caliber machine guns. By June of 1942, eighteen of her .50 caliber mounts had been replaced by thirty-two 20MM single mounts and one 40MM quad had been added to her port quarter. At the same time, a CXAM-1 radar was added. None of this helped against the three torpedos that hit her on 15 September 1942.

WASP's air group ranged from sixty-six to seventy-two aircraft during her short career.

WASP carried a CXAM-1 Air Search Radar and RFD fire control radars on Mk 33 gun directors. WASP had a short operational career, being lost after receiving three torpedo hits on 15 September 1942. (NARA)

WASP

USS WASP at anchor in the Atlantic during March of 1942. She is painted in Measure 12 Mod camouflage. The aircraft with the upward folding wings are SB2U Vindicator scout bombers. (NARA)

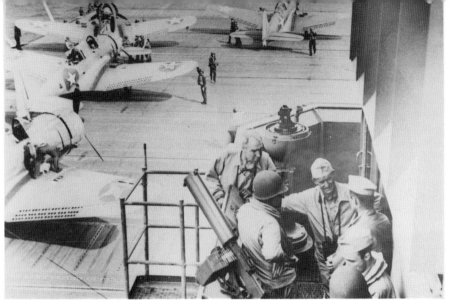

SBDs are spotted forward on WASP after returning from strikes against Guadalcanal on 7 August 1942. A small, water-cooled .30 cal. machine gun is mounted on the bridge rail, more for morale than for defense. (NHC)

The 1.1" quad mounts fitted to WASP during 1941, proved utterly ineffective in combat, and were replaced by the 40mm Bofors as soon as they became available. (NARA)

The starboard side of WASP's flightdeck aft of the island was lined with a battery of water-cooled .50 cal. machine guns. The presence of these light AA guns and the old fashioned helmets worn by the gun crew indicate that this was early in the war. By the time WASP entered combat in the South Pacific, these machine guns had been replaced by the slightly more effective 20mm Oerlikon cannon. (NARA)

Carrier Aircraft

Aircraft carriers are large, complex vessels designed solely to launch, recover, service and repair naval aircraft. While there were significant qualitative differences between aircraft carriers in terms of design, doctrine and training (for example, U.S. aircraft carrier crews had considerably better refueling doctrine and training than their Japanese counterparts, which had a decisive impact on the battle of Midway), eventually an aircraft carrier's combat potential rested in the quality and quantity of its aircraft and aircrews.

For much of the war, U.S. Navy aircraft had a significantly shorter range than their Japanese counterparts. U.S. designers opted for big, tough, heavily armed and armored aircraft with big engines; the Japanese tended to build lighter aircraft that had a significant range and, at least at the beginning of the war, speed advantage over the Americans. The Japanese aircraft, however, were not able to absorb the amount of punishment that the U.S. Navy's aircraft could. This difference in design emphasis was in large part due to the difference in strategic position of the two countries prior to the war. The U.S. had few island possessions in the Pacific and therefore designed its naval aircraft solely for carrier combat; the Japanese had numerous island bases and therefore planned to operate from and between those islands, as well as from aircraft carriers. Since those bases were often far separated, the Japanese considered range among the most essential characteristics of a naval aircraft.

The Japanese started the war with the Mitsubishi A6M Zero as their principal naval fighter. The Zero was fast, light and nimble, lightly armed and almost completely lacking in armor. Its range was in excess of 1,000 nm. The Americans flew the Grumman F4F Wildcat. It was slower, heavier and less maneuverable, but was heavily armed and well armored. Its combat range was barely 500 nm.

These differences in design characteristics affected the carrier war in a number of ways. A number of U.S. sorties, particularly early in the war, were called off because Japanese naval aircraft found U.S. aircraft carriers at distances far beyond the range of American aircraft. The best example of this was LEXINGTON's aborted raid on Rabaul during February 1942. However, once American pilots learned of the relative vulnerability of the Japanese aircraft, they found out that they could often attack with relative impunity, counting on the enemy aircraft to disintegrate long before it could inflict critical damage in return. One Japanese aircraft, the twin-engine Mitsubishi G4M bomber (code-named Betty) became so notoriously easy to set on fire that it was nick-named "Ronson" by U.S. pilots.

U.S. Navy aircraft before the war were extremely colorful. Upper wing surfaces were Chrome Yellow, the tail was in the carrier identification color (in this case, Blue for ENTERPRISE) and the cowl ring, wing and fuselage stripes indicated the section (in this case, Lemon Yellow). This TBD was assigned to the 6th section of VT-6 (NHC)

Shortly before the outbreak of war, the Navy had adopted a much drabber finish, Intermediate Blue Gray over Light Gray with national insignia carried in six positions and thirteen Red and White stripes on the rudder. An F4F-3 on ENTERPRISE has its guns bore sighted while a dark canvas cover hides the rudder stripes. (NHC)

Brewster F2A Buffalo

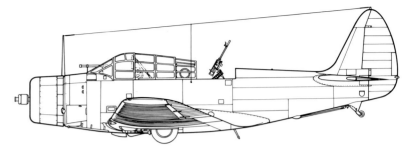

Douglas TBD Devastator

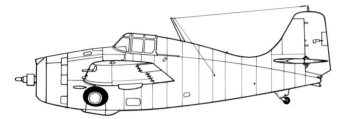

Grumman F4F Wildcat

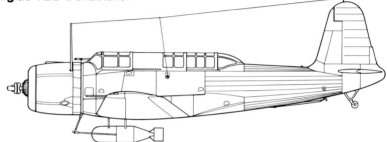

Vought SB2U Vindicator

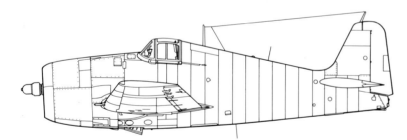

Grumman F6F Hellcat

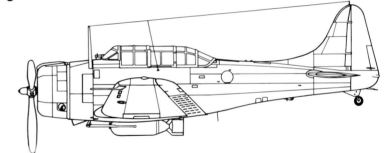

Douglas SBD Dauntless

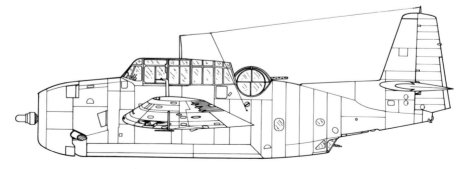

Grumman TBF Avenger

36

Navy carriers also served to deliver U.S. Army Air Corps fighters to the front. These Curtiss P-40F Warhawks prepare to fly off RANGER on 19 July 1942. (NARA)

These SBD Dauntless dive bombers being respotted on ENTERPRISE on 3 May 1942 have enlarged wing insignia. The wing insignia was gradually increased in size in an attempt to improve recognition, particularly by surface anti-aircraft gunners. (NARA)

An F4F-4 went over the side of RANGER on 25 August 1942. The problem of friendly fire was finally solved by removing the Red from the insignia and the rudder stripes. Because the Japanese roundel was Red, surface AA gunners fired at any aircraft with Red markings. (NHC)

A forklift is pressed into service as an aircraft tractor to reposition this Avenger on 19 November 1943. Instead of a tow bar, ropes were attached to the main landing gear.

A variety of deck equipment was used to move aircraft and their weapons around the flight deck such as this hand trolley, which was used to move 500 pound bombs from the magazine to waiting Douglas SBD Dauntless dive bombers aboard RANGER, during November of 1942.

Aircraft tractors tow F4F Wildcats by their tailwheels aboard RANGER on 10 October 1942. Each aircraft has a safety walker assigned to ensure that no damage comes to the aircraft while it is being towed. (NARA)

A Hellcat is motioned forward by a deck crewman prior to take-off from SARATOGA on 20 November 1943. The VFs were always the first off the deck because they needed much less deck to get airborne than the bigger and more heavily loaded VTs or VSBs. (NARA)

Late in the war, the multi-colored camouflage schemes gave way to an overall Gloss Sea Blue camouflage. The ENTERPRISE air group, embarked on 16 October 1944, was made up of F6F Hellcats, TBM Avengers and SB2C Helldivers, all in overall Gloss Sea Blue. (NARA)

Fighter Control Radars

A number of the carrier air battles during 1942 were characterized, on the American side, by a breakdown in control of the defensive Combat Air Patrol (CAP) allowing the Japanese to get in attacks that might have otherwise been stopped. There were a number of reasons for this, most having to do with radio discipline and training. One reason, at least, was technological, namely that the air-search radars of the time lacked a height-finding capability. On more than one occasion fighters were vectored correctly, but at the wrong altitude.

The obvious solution was narrow beam radar mounted so as to scan vertically as well as rotating. The first of these was the SM (originally CXBL) which first was mounted on U.S. aircraft carriers during 1943. SM was an S-band radar fitted with an eight foot diameter circular dish antenna. The SM's mounting was heavy, restricting its use to fleet carriers. Later, it was superseded by the smaller SP radar with a six foot diameter antenna. Both of these antennas appeared in a variety of forms: they could be full circles or circles with an arc section removed at the bottom or both bottom and top. Also, they were almost always fitted with the dipole antennas of the BO IFF system, which could be mounted on three parallel vertical rails mounted in front of the dish, on a separate mattress antenna mounted above the dish or both.

SM Radar Antenna

Combat

At the time of the Japanese attack on Pearl Harbor, the U.S. Navy's aircraft carriers were deployed as follows: LANGLEY, LEXINGTON, SARATOGA and ENTERPRISE were in the Pacific while RANGER, YORKTOWN, WASP & HORNET were in the Atlantic. HORNET was not yet fully operational and was still working up.

Some of the ships had already seen action. RANGER had been operating from the newly acquired base at Bermuda since April, 1941, as part of the Central Atlantic Neutrality Patrol, transferring to the North Atlantic Patrol on 1 September. The Neutrality Patrol was a device invented by FDR to assist the Royal Navy during 1941 without the inconvenience of a declaration of war. The U.S. Navy took over convoy escort duties in the Western Atlantic, freeing up the Royal Navy's hard pressed escort groups for the critical battle in the Western Approaches.

WASP joined TG 7.3 operating from Bermuda during June. She carried a deckload of P-40s to Iceland, flying them off on 19 July. Then on 1 September, she joined the Denmark Straits Patrol. On 10 November, RANGER joined the escort of a critical convoy, WS 12, from Halifax, which she escorted as far as 17° S, where the Royal Navy took over.

In the Pacific, the U.S. Navy saw the approach of war and prepared as well as it could. Contrary to legend, the attack on Pearl Harbor was a surprise only as to where it was delivered. The timing and enemy were no surprise. The active aircraft carriers were all being used to carry aircraft reinforcements to isolated island outposts. ENTERPRISE set out from Pearl Harbor with a deckload of Marine F4F Wildcats for Wake, flying them off on 4 December 1941.

Meanwhile, LEXINGTON was enroute to Midway, flying off her deckload of Marine F2A Buffalos on 7 December, almost at the same time that the Japanese were attacking Pearl Harbor. That day, ENTERPRISE was approaching Pearl Harbor on her return from Wake. As was normal practice on approaching home base, the ENTERPRISE air group was to fly off while the carrier was still some distance at sea. The lead element of her air group was eighteen SBDs of VB-6 and VS-6 that were sent out to cover scouting sectors ahead of the carrier. These flights would carry them out some 250 nm and, after completing their sweeps, they would head towards Pearl Harbor rather that return to the carrier. The ones that were sent out on either side of the ship's track had relatively uneventful sweeps, but those that scouted ahead of ENTERPRISE arrived over Oahu at the same time as the first wave of Japanese attackers. Some were lost to Zeros and those that survived the Japanese became targets for trigger happy American gunners on the ground. Before the morning was over, five of ENTERPRISE's SBDs were lost to the Japanese and one to friendly fire.

What was significant about the attack was not what was lost, but rather what was not lost. By pure luck, none of the three active Pacific Fleet carriers were in port at Pearl Harbor that day. As a result, the ships and their air groups remained essentially intact. The only significant response to the attack was by the ENTERPRISE air group. Searches for the now retiring Japanese were launched both from Pearl Harbor and by ENTERPRISE SBDs, but it was far too late. What was evident that afternoon, and what would became increasingly evident over the next few months, was that aircraft carriers now represented the primary striking force available to Pacific Fleet.

Once the initial shock of the Japanese attack had worn off, the primary concern of Pacific Fleet planners was for conservation of those assets that remained undamaged and defense against the expected follow-on attacks by the Japanese. Because there was no way of being certain the Japanese wouldn't return to Pearl Harbor to finish the job, Pacific Fleet's aircraft carriers spent as little time in port as possible. An integral part of

A mushroom cloud rises over LEXINGTON after an AVGAS (Aviation Gasoline) explosion ripped through her hull. The damage from the Japanese bombs and torpedos was not fatal in itself, but once the leaking AVGAS caught fire, her fate was sealed. (NHC)

the conservative strategy adopted by Pacific Fleet planners was a continuation of the effort to beef up U.S. island bases.

On 14 December, LEXINGTON set out from Pearl Harbor, followed two days later by SARATOGA. LEXINGTON was to carry out a raid on Jaluit in the Marshalls, diverting Japanese attention from the real intent of the mission, SARATOGA's delivery of eighteen F2A Buffalos to Wake. The Japanese, however, were moving faster than the Americans. Wake Island had already successfully resisted one attack, but the Japanese returned in force on 21 December, reinforced by two aircraft carriers from the Pearl Harbor strike force. The Jaluit diversion was hastily cancelled and LEXINGTON rerouted to the North. SARATOGA was ordered to make best speed, but she failed to arrive in position to launch a strike before the Marine garrison on Wake was overwhelmed on 23 December. The entire mission was cancelled that same day and both aircraft carriers recalled to Pearl Harbor.

The whole experience left a bad taste. There had been indecision and poor execution from the beginning of the operation. Changes were needed. Most fundamental was a change in command at CINCPACFLT (Commander-in-Chief Pacific Fleet). ADM Kimmel, rendered almost immobile by accusations that he was responsible for the disaster at Pearl Harbor, was replaced by ADM Chester Nimitz. Reinforcements were on their way as well. YORKTOWN was dispatched from the Atlantic, scheduled to arrive at Pearl Harbor during early January. HORNET would join the Pacific Fleet as soon as her work ups in the Atlantic were completed.

On 11 January 1942, SARATOGA was torpedoed by the Japanese fleet submarine I-6 near Pearl Harbor. This left the Pacific Fleet with three operational aircraft carriers. SARATOGA wasn't seriously damaged but was laid up at San Diego for repairs and would not be ready for action until 1 June. LANGLEY, was lost in an attack by Japanese land-based naval aircraft on 27 February while attempting to deliver P-40 reinforcements to Java. She was lost during 1942, a year that was to be, in real terms, by far the most serious in U.S. naval history, far more diastrous than 1941. By the end of the year, only three of the eight U.S. Navy carriers would still be afloat.

During 1942, Pacific Fleet, under ADM Nimitz, took on a new sense of purpose. At first that purpose was vengeance! The sense of frustration and powerlessness left by the Pearl Harbor raid and the failure to save Wake, left the Pacific Fleet with an overwhelming desire to strike back at the Japanese in almost any fashion. The first missions of the new year were inspired by a desire to strike at the Japanese at a variety of points in order to keep them off balance. Admittedly, no one thought that these small scale raids would do serious damage to the enemy, but if they diverted Japanese attention from the present weakness of the Allied forces, particularly in the South Pacific, then they would be worthwhile. If they slowed down the Japanese advance to any extent, made them a bit more cautious, then they were beneficial. Everyone at Pearl Harbor knew that victory would eventually be theirs. Time and superior numbers would inevitably win the war. Slowing the Japanese down now would make that eventual victory come sooner and at lower cost.

The sequence of these raids on the Japanese periphery was to begin with LEXINGTON hitting Wake. The raid was aborted when, on 23 January, a day after leaving Pearl Harbor, one of the accompanying oilers was sunk by the Japanese submarine I-72. Instead, the process began with raids on the Marshalls and Gilberts by ENTERPRISE and YORKTOWN, which joined at Samoa on 25 January. Thirty-seven aircraft from the YORKTOWN air group carried out raids on Jaluit, Mili and Makin on 1 February, losing six aircraft. On the same day, ENTERPRISE attacked Wotje, Maloelap and Kwajelein with sixty-four aircraft attacking in two waves, also losing six. The results of these raids was minor, one cruiser and one minelayer damaged. In turn, ENTERPRISE was slightly damaged by counterattacking Japanese land-based aircraft. Both task forces returned directly to Pearl Harbor, leaving again as soon as they could replenish. ENTERPRISE left Pearl Harbor on 14 February enroute to Wake and Marcus while YORKTOWN left two days later to raid Eniwetok in the Marshalls. ENTERPRISE carried out her planned raid on Wake with twenty-four aircraft on 24 February and then went on to attack Marcus on 4 March.

YORKTOWN, however, never carried out her scheduled raid. Instead, she was recalled before getting to Eniwetok, being diverted to escort a high-priority convoy to the South Pacific, arriving at Noumea at the end of February. This move represented a significant change in strategic emphasis for Pacific Fleet, because LEXINGTON had already made the same move to the South Pacific. She has left Pearl Harbor on 31 January, escorting an earlier convoy via Bora Bora to the New Hebrides. LEXINGTON started operations in the South Pacific on 17 February, leaving Noumea to carry out a raid on Rabaul.

She was found and attacked by Japanese land-based naval aircraft well before she was in range of Rabaul. As a result, LEXINGTON called off the Rabaul operation and, after refueling, sortied into the Coral Sea. The Coral Sea was bounded on the East by the Solomon Islands, on the North by New Guinea and on the West by Australia, making it a highly valuable stretch of water. LEXINGTON joined YORKTOWN near Noumea on 6 March and the two aircraft carriers moved North together, heading for New Guinea to raid Japanese-held positions on the Papuan Peninsula. On 10 April, 104 aircraft from the two carriers flew over the Owen Stanley Mountains for attacks on Lae and Salamaua. As in previous perimeter raids, the results failed to live up to the risks: one transport was sunk and a number of small warships and auxiliaries were damaged.

One more small raid on the Japanese was to follow, but this one was definitely not a raid on the Japanese perimeter. On 2 April 1942, HORNET, having just completed her work ups, left San Francisco with an unusual deckload of aircraft. In place of her normal air group, she carried a deckload of Army Air Corps B-25 Mitchell bombers. The target this time was Japan itself. To protect HORNET, which was essentially defenseless with her deck full of bombers, ENTERPRISE was assigned escort duty, leaving Pearl Harbor on 8 April. The two task forces joined up on 13 April. On the 18th, still some miles to the East of the intended launch point, the ships were sighted by Japanese picket boats and faced with the decision to abort, to push on to the planned launch point against an alerted enemy or to launch immediately with full knowledge that the B-25s lacked the range to

The light carrier SHOHO, on fire aft but still moving at high speed, was caught by two carrier air groups on the morning of 7 May 1942. The attack was called off when the ship was dead in the water and sinking by the stern. The success was reported back to the U.S. carriers with the famous message: "Scratch one flattop!" (NHC)

By 1630 that day, the fight against the fires in LEXINGTON was lost. The ship had drifted to a stop and the decision was made to abandon ship. The heavy cruiser NEW ORLEANS pulled alongside in order to shorten the distance that the rescue boats had to cover. (NHC)

LCDR Ito, who led the seventeen Betty bombers that attacked LEXINGTON off Bougainville on 20 February 1942, crashed in flames near his intended target. The left engine had been shot away by Butch O'Hare, who was primarily responsible for breaking up the Japanese attack. LEXINGTON survived this early raid without damage. (NARA)

Crewmen on LEXINGTON survey the damage done to the port forward 5" gun battery by one of the few Japanese bombs to hit LEXINGTON at Coral Sea on 8 May 1942. The bombs caused only minor damage, however, the main damage was done by a single torpedo hit forward. (NARA)

LEXINGTON's air group is positioned aft, refueled and ready to go, but the series of explosions that would eventually sink the old lady had already started and there was no way to launch the aircraft. Smoke is rising from around the periphery of the small amidships elevator. (NHC)

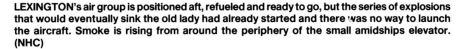

reach their intended landing fields in China. The Army commander, LTC James Doolittle, decided to launch immediately, leading his sixteen Mitchell bombers on raids that hit Tokyo, Nagoya and Kobe. The damage they did was insignificant, but the psychological effect was tremendous. Five Japanese aircraft carriers gave chase but were unable to locate ENTERPRISE and HORNET, which arrived back at Pearl Harbor on 25 April.

The five Pacific Fleet aircraft carriers were deployed as follows: two in the South Pacific, two at Pearl Harbor and one in San Diego under repair. The other two active U.S. Navy aircraft carriers were in the Atlantic. WASP was kept busy escorting convoys until 25 March, when she was sent from her East Coast base at Casco Bay, Maine, with the new battleship USS WASHINGTON, to join up with Royal Navy units at Scapa Flow. The two U.S. warships were to replace Royal Navy units that were temporarily detached to escort troop transports for the invasion of Madagascar.

On 14 April, WASP joined Force W leaving Greenock for Gibraltar, carrying forty-seven Spitfires intended for Malta. She passed Gibraltar into the Mediterranean on the 19th and, the next day, flew off the fighters to Malta. A similar mission was performed between 3 and 9 May, after which WASP returned to Scapa Flow. She was reassigned from Atlantic Fleet to Pacific Fleet shortly thereafter, transiting the Panama Canal on 10 June 1942. RANGER, being older and slower than WASP, was almost never used for combat operations. Most of her time was spent in aircraft transport or convoy escort duty. For example, RANGER, on 10 May and again on 19 July, flew off deckloads of Army P-40s for Accra. In November 1942, she saw her only combat duty of the war when she formed part of the air support for the Operation TORCH landings in North Africa. Her closest brush with mortal danger came on 10 November when the Vichy submarine LE TONNANT fired a torpedo at her — which missed.

On 1 May 1942, the two carriers in the South Pacific, LEXINGTON and YORKTOWN, once again sortied into the Coral Sea. This time it was in response to enemy movements. The relative quiet that had followed the initial Japanese expansion had come to an end. The first of the new Japanese offensive moves was an attempt to land troops on the South coast of the Papuan Peninsula and on Tulagi in the Solomons. At Tulagi, they were to establish a seaplane base that would allow aerial reconnaissance of the essential Allied supply routes to Australia. If unopposed, the move would threaten that lifeline through Samoa, Figi and New Caledonia and eventually threaten Australia itself.

The Japanese supported the troop movements with a sortie by the light carrier SHOHO and the large fleet carriers SHOKAKU and ZUIKAKU. LEXINGTON and YORKTOWN moved into the Coral Sea to oppose these movements. The Japanese carried out landings on Tulagi on 3 May 1942. The next day, the landing party was attacked by ninety-nine aircraft from the two American carriers, sinking a destroyer and three minesweepers and damaging four other ships. The Americans then retired to the Southwest to refuel.

Now alerted to the presence of the U.S. carriers, the Japanese entered the Coral Sea from the East on 5 May. The two forces looked for, but missed each other on the 6th, although at times they were as little as 70 nm apart. On the morning of 7 May, the Americans found the Japanese covering force, including SHOHO, and the Japanese found the U.S. support group. In a series of sharp attacks, U.S. fliers bombed SHOHO, while the Japanese sank the oiler USS NEOSHO and the destroyer USS SIMS. Finally, on the morning of 8 May 1942, the two main carriers forces, each two carriers strong, found each other and launched full strength attacks. YORKTOWN received significant damage, with one bomb passing through the flight deck and exploding in the hangar bay. This hit caused minor damage, but the Japanese has scored no fewer than eleven near-misses, springing hull plates and causing numerous leaks.

SHOKAKU took three bombs that caused a gasoline fire and tore up her flight deck

New ships worked up in the Atlantic prior to deployment to the Pacific front. The battleship NORTH CAROLINA and the aircraft carrier HORNET conduct a training cruise during January of 1942. HORNET would have one of the shortest careers in U.S. Navy history, lasting barely ten months. (NARA)

forward, effectively knocking her out of the battle. It was LEXINGTON, however, that took the worst beating. Hit by torpedos along her port side during the initial Japanese attack and by bombs during the next attack, she was still capable of making 25 knots and operating aircraft. Nevertheless, she was taking water by the bow and fighting a small but persistent fire in her hangar bay. Despite this, her problems seemed to be under control and her captain expected her to stay in the fight when, at 1247, she was whacked by a massive internal explosion, apparently the result of accumulated gasoline vapors from a ruptured avgas tank being detonated by a spark from one of her generators.

HORNET arrived in the Pacific in time to participate in the famous Doolittle raid on Japan. No sooner had she returned to Pearl Harbor from that duty than she was hastily transferred to the South Pacific along with ENTERPRISE. HORNET steams in line behind ENTERPRISE, two oilers and two destroyers on 3 May 1942. The ships arrived too late to take part in the battle of Coral Sea. (NARA)

Amazingly, LEXINGTON continued to operate aircraft for two more hours, but finally the fires made the machinery spaces too hot to man and, once the boiler rooms were abandoned, the fight against the fires was lost. At approximately 1600, a second massive explosion ripped through the hangar deck. By 1630, the ship was dead in the water and by 1707 the fight was lost and the order given to abandon ship. LEXINGTON was finally scuttled by American torpedos at 2000 to prevent her from falling into Japanese hands. By the next morning, the Coral Sea was empty of opposing warships.

The battle of the Coral Sea was important for a number of reasons. This was the first naval battle fought exclusively by the aircraft carriers and carrier aircraft of opposing navies. For the first time, a naval battle had been fought during which the surface ships of the opposing sides never came in sight of each other. For the U.S., Coral Sea was a strategic draw. The Japanese move into the Solomons was slowed, but not stopped. The issue of control of the South Pacific was far from decided. Far more serious, in the short term, was the balance of power in the Pacific. With SHOKAKU damaged and ZUIKAKU's air group decimated, the Japanese still had four effective fleet aircraft carriers. With LEXINGTON sunk and YORKTOWN damaged, the U.S. Navy was down to two aircraft carriers until YORKTOWN and SARATOGA could complete repairs and WASP arrived from the Atlantic.

At this low point in U.S. aircraft carrier strength, a new threat loomed. Excellent work

Only three bombs hit ENTERPRISE, all impacting aft. This bomb hit aft of the island. The fact that the bomb exploding on the flight deck indicates that its fuse has misfired. Naval bombs were normally fitted with delayed action fuses that allowed them to penetrate to a lower deck; this bomb did little damage. (NHC)

breaking Japanese codes allowed U.S. Navy Intelligence to identify the next Japanese offensive move. This time it was to be a major thrust straight across the Pacific to Midway Island, the farthest West of a series of atolls that extended to the Northwest of the Hawaiian chain. It lay just 1,250 nm from Pearl Harbor. Along the way, the Japanese hoped to draw the U.S. Navy into that major naval battle for control of the Pacific. The Japanese were loyal disciples of ADM Mahan and believed that they must fight and win this battle in order to force the U.S. to accept defeat. They knew the U.S. Navy would have to react to a threat against Midway because loss of the island and the establishment of a Japanese base there would force the Pacific Fleet out of Pearl Harbor and back to the West Coast. What they didn't know was that the U.S. Navy was "reading their mail."

The U.S. reaction was, naturally enough, to concentrate all available forces near Midway. Unfortunately, it was pathetically small concentration. ENTERPRISE and HORNET, back from the Tokyo raid, had been rushed to the South Pacific but arrived too late for Coral Sea. Now they retraced their route, were resupplied and left Pearl Harbor for Midway on 28 May. YORKTOWN was rushed at best speed from the South Pacific, arriving at Pearl Harbor on 27 May, where she was immediately drydocked. Looking at YORKTOWN's condition, the repair crew estimated it would take several weeks to perform the needed work — Nimitz gave them 24 hours. Thus, on 28 May, only hours after ENTERPRISE and HORNET, YORKTOWN also left Pearl Harbor for Midway. The work remaining on SARATOGA was also hurried and she too was rushed to the area, but she was not able to leave San Diego until 1 June. WASP was only just approaching the Atlantic side of the Panama Canal and would be unable to reach Midway in time. The aircraft carriers already on the way would have to be enough.

The three aircraft carriers converging on Midway reached the area on 2 June 1942, just two days before the Japanese arrived. The Japanese started the action with a significant disadvantage: they had divided objectives. Their aircraft carriers were there to support the occupation of Midway. Their secondary mission was to find and defeat the American carriers. As a result, their first strike at dawn on 4 June was against the island, hitting the Marine defenders with a total of 108 aircraft. A similar number was reserved on the Japanese decks in case the enemy aircraft carriers were spotted.

The Japanese mounted a minimal search by float planes, but the single aircraft assigned the sector in which the U.S. carriers were located was late being launched. Meanwhile, the Americans took full advantage of their possession of Midway Island, locating and attacking the Japanese carriers with land-based aircraft as the U.S. carriers

WASP fell victim to the same fate as LEXINGTON. Hit by torpedos, she was wracked by successive Avgas explosions. Her captain tried steaming backwards in a futile attempt to confine the fires. WASP sank much faster than LEXINGTON, being abandoned just thirty-five minutes after the torpedos hit. (NARA)

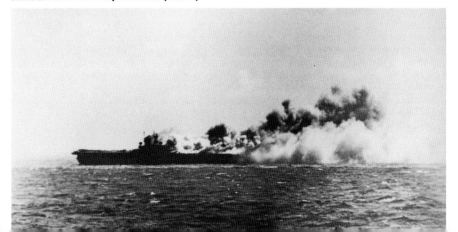

approached at high speed from the East. The first Japanese attack on Midway failed to silence the island's defenses. ADM Nagumo, the Japanese commander, made a serious mistake opting to rearm his deckload of aircraft for land attack rather than strike them below or launch them in order to clear his decks for the returning first strike. Not too surprisingly, the rearming process was still going on when the first wave returned.

Nagumo now faced a poor set of choices. He could complete the rearming process and launch his deckload of attack aircraft, but that would risk the loss of many of the first aircraft which were running low on fuel. He could launch those aircraft to clear his decks, land and strike below the first wave and then recover the second strike and complete the rearming process, but that would delay the launching of the second strike for hours. Finally, he could strike those aircraft below, land the first wave and then refuel and rearm the first wave aircraft on deck. This third option would allow a second attack to be launched sooner than the second choice, but it would leave his carriers with a hangar full of fueled and partially armed aircraft while the rest of his aircraft were being fueled and armed on deck for the next attack on Midway. This third option was by far the most dangerous for his carriers, since they would be extraordinarily vulnerable. It was this option that Nagumo chose. This process was partially complete when word came from the delayed scout that the U.S. carriers had been sighted. Now Nagumo had to choose whether to complete the arming process for the attack on Midway or remove the high explosive bombs from his aircraft and rearm them for a strike at the American aircraft carriers. He chose the latter course.

Despite all these blunders, the Japanese came within minutes of getting off a massive strike at the U.S. carriers. Their carriers were turning into the wind just as American SBD dive bombers arrived overhead. Within minutes, three of the four Japanese aircraft carriers were on fire and sinking. Caught with their decks full of fueled and armed aircraft, they were doomed as soon as the first bomb exploded. Only HIRYU survived the onslaught and only because she was some distance from the other three and wasn't seen by the Americans. HIRYU was able to launch two small attacks. Both found YORKTOWN. The first put three bombs into her and started fires which were soon brought under control. The second wave hit YORKTOWN with two torpedos and this led to her being abandoned. Later in the day, aircraft from ENTERPRISE and HORNET found HIRYU and added her to the list of sinking Japanese aircraft carriers.

When, the next morning, YORKTOWN was still afloat, small crews were sent back aboard to get her under tow and to fight the remaining fires. By 8 June, it looked as though she could be saved and further crew was put aboard to try to raise steam. At this point, the Japanese submarine I-168 decided her fate, putting two more torpedos into her. This time the flooding could not be halted and the next morning, 9 June 1942, YORKTOWN capsized and sank.

In the aftermath of the Battle of Midway, the strategic picture in the Pacific had completely changed. Now the U.S. had four fleet aircraft carriers in the theater (counting WASP and SARATOGA) while the Japanese were reduced to two (although they had one large merchant conversion working up (JUNYO) and a second (HIYO) nearing completion). A major effort by the Japanese to capture the New Hebrides, Fiji and Samoa scheduled for July had to be cancelled. Nevertheless, smaller advances continued, including the construction of an airfield opposite Tulagi on the island of Guadalcanal. The Americans were determined to keep the Japanese from finishing this airfield because land-based reconnaissance aircraft operating from Guadalcanal would be far more dangerous than the float planes at Tulagi. Rather than just bomb it into submission, ADM Nimitz decided that it would be far better to take it over and use it against its former owners.

U.S. Marines landed on Guadalcanal on 7 August 1942, starting a campaign that

On 26 October 1942, during the Battle of Santa Cruz, ENTERPRISE had SOUTH DAKOTA (background) in her screen, adding greatly to the volume of AA fire. The smoke rising in the background is from the destroyer USS SMITH (DD 378) which was hit by a Kate diving on ENTERPRISE. (NHC)

would continue well into the next year. Both sides realized that there was far more at stake than a jungle airstrip. Rather, they were fighting for the initiative in the South Pacific. The winning side would pick the time and place for the next battle. Eventually, both sides committed all of their aircraft carrier resources to this critical campaign.

The initial landings were supported by ENTERPRISE, WASP and SARATOGA. The Japanese reaction was to bring SHOKAKU and ZUIKAKU, along with the small carrier RYUJO down to Truk (in the Carolines) and then, on 23 August, into the waters east of the Solomons in support of a reinforcement convoy. The three U.S. aircraft carriers entered the same waters from the south on the same day. Reconnaissance aircraft from Henderson Field (the new name for the airstrip on Guadalcanal) found the Japanese troop transports. The air group from SARATOGA was assigned the task of attacking the troopships that afternoon but, in the event, they failed to find their targets and landed at Henderson Field for the night. WASP, running low on fuel, retired to the south that evening to replenish. She would miss the battle coming the next day.

In the morning of 24 August 1942, SARATOGA's air group returned and both carriers sent out reconnaissance sweeps searching for the Japanese carriers. The Japanese were arrayed much as they had been at Coral Sea, with small RYUJO in advance of the two larger carriers to act as a scout and, if necessary, a sacrificial lamb. American reconnaissance patrols found RYUJO, which became the target of a nearly full strike off SARATOGA and ENTERPRISE. SARATOGA's air group found RYUJO first, putting at least four bombs and one torpedo hit into the small aircraft carrier. They left her a blazing wreck. ENTERPRISE's strike never found the target, but it wasn't needed; RYUJO was sinking.

In the meantime, Japanese scouts found the American carriers and the two large Japanese carriers launched a relatively small strike which, nevertheless, was able to put three bombs into ENTERPRISE, temporarily putting her out of action. Both sides launched further strikes which failed to find each other as the day drew to a close. Under the cover of night, both sides withdrew to refuel and assess damage. The Japanese had lost another small carrier and once again had failed to deliver a decisive blow, but their two remaining carriers were unharmed and their air groups were largely intact. The U.S. still had both carriers, but ENTERPRISE had been hit hard enough to require a visit to

Maneuvering violently, in a largely successful attempt to avoid Japanese bombers, ENTERPRISE pitched steeply to starboard. The maneuver caused a Douglas SBD Dauntless to slip into the starboard gallery aft. (NARA)

When the SBD went into the gallery deck, there was no choice but to shove the aircraft over the side to clear the deck for other aircraft. There was no time to mount a salvage operation to recover the Dauntless. (NARA)

the dry dock at Pearl Harbor. This inconclusive engagement became known as the Battle of the Eastern Solomons.

In the next two weeks, Japanese submarines accomplished what ADM Nagumo's carriers had been unable to achieve. On 31 August 1942, while operating in the Coral Sea, SARATOGA was torpedoed for the second time in less than eight months. Only one, out of a spread of six, fired by I-26 actually hit SARATOGA. The flooding was minor, but it was enough to short out her turbo-electric drive and leave her dead in the water. Once again she faced a slow transit back to the West Coast and months in dry dock. Barely two weeks later an even more devastating blow was struck by I-19 which, with one spread of six torpedos, damaged the battleship NORTH CAROLINA, fatally wounded the destroyer O'BRIEN and hit WASP three times. She was caught by the torpedos while refueling aircraft, a very vulnerable state for an aircraft carrier. Fires from burning aircraft and ruptured Avgas lines soon turned the front half of the ship into an inferno. In just thirty-five minutes the fires were so far beyond control that WASP had to abandoned. After burning the rest of the day, she was scuttled that night. One torpedo from that salvo had come close to hitting HORNET, newly arrived in the South Pacific to replace SARATOGA.

Suddenly, the power equation was tipped against the U.S. Until 16 October, when ENTERPRISE would leave Pearl Harbor to return to the South Pacific, HORNET was the only operational U.S. aircraft carrier in the Pacific. Since RANGER was inadequate for Pacific operations, there would be no reinforcements for months to come.

In ENTERPRISE's absence, HORNET was kept busy in the South Pacific, carrying out a raid on the Shortlands on 5 October 1942 and providing distant escort to yet another reinforcement convoy to Guadalcanal four days later. While this was going on, the Japanese were preparing another major reinforcement of their own. Their two big aircraft carriers, SHOKAKU and ZUIKAKU, now joined by the light carrier ZUIHO, came along to provide distant escort while the merchant conversion JUNYO provided close escort to the reinforcement convoy. These forces moved into the waters east of Guadalcanal on 26 October 1942.

HORNET, joined just in time by the repaired ENTERPRISE, came into the same waters from the southeast. The resulting engagement was known as the Battle of Santa Cruz. Japanese search planes found HORNET at 0730 at a distance of only 185 nm. SBD scouts found ADM Nagumo's ships twenty minutes later. The Americans struck first when one of the bomb-armed scouts put a 500 pound bomb into ZUIHO's flight deck. This single attack didn't stop the Japanese from getting off two large waves of attack aircraft. Before the first of these arrived over the American ships, the U.S. carriers had launched their own strikes, meaning that the two sides would make their attacks at about the same time.

Her luck running true, ENTERPRISE found a small rain squall to hide in just as the first wave of Japanese aircraft arrived overhead. This left HOTNET to bear the brunt of the attack. The first wave put four bombs and two torpedos into HORNET. One of the torpedos flooded her forward engine room, bringing HORNET to a stop, while the bombs left her with small fires forward. Meanwhile, the American strike put between three and six bombs into SHOKAKU, gutting her hangar deck but leaving her still capable of steaming. The second wave of Japanese aircraft found ENTERPRISE and hit her with two bombs, while a third was a near miss; even so, she remained fully operational. By 1600, HORNET had spent five hours repairing damage, rerouting steam piping around the flooded engine room, and was preparing to get underway again when the last Japanese strike found her and put a single torpedo into her after engine room. This single blow sealed her fate, since it was now impossible to make way under her own power or to even run the pumps that were keeping the flooding under control. There remained no other option but to scuttle her before Japanese surface ships arrived. U.S. destroyers put a number of torpedos into the hulk and fled the scene. HORNET was still afloat, however, when Japanese destroyers arrived, but she was so far gone that they had no choice but to finish the job with their own torpedos.

Until SARATOGA returned in January 1943, ENTERPRISE was now the sole U.S. aircraft carrier in the Pacific. Her damage at Santa Cruz had been so minor that, by 1 November, she was back at work escorting reinforcements to Guadalcanal. The Japanese had two aircraft carriers, ZUIKAKU and JUNYO, still undamaged, but their losses of aircrews had been so great at Santa Cruz that it would be many months before they would consider further offensive action. The Japanese aircrew losses turned out to be more serious than that. Unlike the Americans, the Japanese had failed to train new aircrew to replace the inevitable losses in experienced pilots. As a result, the Japanese never recovered from the losses in the carriers battles of 1942.

ENTERPRISE mounted the last carrier operation of the Guadalcanal campaign on 13 and 14 November 1942, when her aircraft helped sink the Japanese battleship HIEI after the first naval battle of Guadalcanal and then sank the cruiser KINUGASA and damaged other cruisers in the last major Japanese effort to hold the island. Not too long after, the Japanese decided to abandon Guadalcanal: the cost in ships had just become too great. With that decision, the intensity seemed to be turned down a notch in the carrier war. Compared to 1942, 1943 would be very quiet. With the new year, the two surviving U.S. aircraft carriers in the Pacific (SARATOGA and ENTERPRISE) were gradually supplemented by the light carrier conversions (on heavy cruiser hulls) and later by the first units of the ESSEX class fleet carriers.

SARATOGA and ENTERPRISE remained in the South Pacific through February 1943. At that point ENTERPRISE returned stateside for a long overdue overhaul and SARATOGA began a cycle of support for the first of the landings that would take back the islands of the Central Pacific from the Japanese. On 29 June, SARATOGA was teamed up with HMS VICTORIOUS against any possible Japanese reaction to the landings on New Georgia in the Solomons, but, when that expected reaction did not occur, they sent their air groups on attack missions in support of the landings.

During November of 1943, SARATOGA was again in the South Pacific, this time with the light carrier PRINCETON, covering the landings at Torokina on Bougainville. The two aircraft carriers staged raids on the Japanese airstrips at Buna and Buka on 1 and 2 November. On 4 November, they hit Rabaul, damaging six cruisers and a destroyer. The Japanese responded with strong air attacks from Rabaul, leading the two carriers to hit the same target again on 11 November, this time with little effect due to poor visibility. That second raid on Rabaul was joined by aircraft from two new ESSEX class aircraft carriers and a new light carrier. The days of holding the line against the Japanese with a few prewar carriers were rapidly drawing to a close.

SARATOGA and ENTERPRISE were both back in action in the Central Pacific in mid-November, providing support for the landings on Tarawa and Makin. SARATOGA, still teamed with PRINCETON, hit Nauru; ENTERPRISE with the light carriers BELLEAU WOOD and MONTEREY provided direct support to the Marines landing on Makin. On 4 December, ENTERPRISE, along with ESSEX and BELLEAU WOOD, raided Kwajelein. The rate at which the U.S. fast carrier task forces built up during late 1943 was staggering. The Gilberts operations employed SARATOGA, ENTERPRISE, five light carriers and four ESSEX class carriers.

During late 1943, RANGER had the last of her rare opportunities to take part in combat operations. Lent to the Royal Navy's Home Fleet for a raid on Bodo, Norway, on 4 October 1943, the air group from RANGER accounted for four transports against the loss of five aircraft.

While HORNET was successfully fighting the damage caused by two torpedos and at least five bomb hits, she fell victim to a single additional torpedo hit from an attack by nine Kates. The additional damage was enough to doom the carrier. (NARA)

The pace of operations in the Central Pacific picked up quickly during 1944. Both ENTERPRISE and SARATOGA supported the landings in the Marshalls, though again as part of different task groups. SARATOGA operated with PRINCETON and with the new light carrier LANGLEY, raiding Wotje on 29 January. On the same day, ENTERPRISE teamed with the new Essex class carrier YORKTOWN and BELLEAU WOOD to raid Maloelap. Both task groups continued to attack targets in the Marshalls through 6 February. At that time, ENTERPRISE's task group was detached to raid Truk, the major Japanese base in the Central Pacific, on 17 February 1944.

ENTERPRISE returned to the South Pacific during March, supporting landings at Emirau in the Bismarcks on 18 March. After replenishing at Espiritu Santo, ENTERPRISE along with BELLEAU WOOD and two escort carriers carried out raids on Palau, Yap and Woleai in the Palaus and Western Caroline Islands between 30 March and 1 April. On 21 April, ENTERPRISE, now with the new LEXINGTON and light carriers PRINCETON and LANGLEY, raided Hollandia in support of landings held there the next day. On 29 and 30 April, the same task group raided Truk.

While ENTERPRISE was engaged in the South Pacific, SARATOGA was venturing into a new theater, the Indian Ocean. On 27 March 1944, SARATOGA joined up with the Royal Navy's Eastern Fleet southwest of the Cocos Islands and returned with that fleet to its base at Trincomalee, Ceylon, arriving there on 2 April. SARATOGA remained in the Indian Ocean until 18 May, participating in two joint operations. On 19 April, TF 70, comprised of SARATOGA and HMS ILLUSTRIOUS, raided Sabang on Sumatra, sinking one steamer and destroying twenty-four Japanese aircraft. On 17 May, the same task force hit Surabaya, again inflicting minor damage. This time SARATOGA exited the Indian Ocean, on her way back to the states for a long overdue major refit that would keep her out of action until February 1945.

ENTERPRISE returned to operations in the Central Pacific with the invasion of the Mariannas. She raided Saipan and Tinian on 11, 12 and 13 June 1944 and then withdrew to replenish. She was back in time to participate in the Battle of the Philippine Sea, the last great aircraft carrier battle of the war. The Japanese had been conserving their forces, anticipating this American move to breach the Mariannas barrier and threw their entire aircraft carrier fleet against ADM Mitscher's Task Force 58.

The Japanese force consisted of three fleet aircraft carriers (SHOKAKU, ZUIKAKU and the new TAIHO), four light carriers and the large merchant conversions HIYO and JUNYO. Against them, TF 58 arrayed seven fleet carriers (ENTERPRISE plus the Essex class carriers HORNET, LEXINGTON, YORKTOWN, WASP, ESSEX and BUNKER HILL) and eight light carriers. Not only were the Japanese seriously outnumbered, but the quality of their aircraft and pilots, compared to the Americans, had badly deteriorated since the early days of the war. Japanese reconnaissance found the American carriers on 19 June 1944 and launched a strike of some 372 aircraft. Of this number, 242 were shot down by F6F Hellcats long before they got close to TF 58. This massacre became known as the Great Mariannas Turkey Shoot.

The Americans failed to locate the Japanese carriers that day because the Japanese had launched at extreme range, planning to use Guam as a refueling stop. U.S. submarines found the Japanese, however, sinking TAIHO and the veteran SHOKAKU. U.S. carrier aircraft did not find the Japanese until the afternoon of the next day, as they were withdrawing. ADM Mitscher launched 216 aircraft despite the extreme range and late hour. These sank HIYO and the light carrier CHIYODA; twenty aircraft were lost in the attack and seventy-two others ditched or crash landed due to fuel exhaustion.

ENTERPRISE was next in action on 31 August, carrying out a series of raids on Iwo and Chichi Jima that lasted three days. This time, she was teamed with the ESSEX class aircraft carrier FRANKLIN and the light carrier SAN JACINTO as part of TG 38.4. (TF 58 and TF 38 were the same force; it simply changed its number when ADM Spruance (58) or ADM Halsey (38) was in charge). They then began a series of raids in the Palaus, starting on 6 September, in support of landings there. The ENTERPRISE task group remained in the Palaus for the rest of the month, while the rest of TF 38 carried out raids throughout the Philippines in preparation for the landings on Leyte scheduled for October.

On 7 October, TG 38.4 rejoined the rest of TF 38 for a sortie against Formosa and Northern Luzon. ENTERPRISE's aircraft hit targets on Formosa on 10 October, Aparri airfield on Luzon on the 11th, Formosa on the 12th and 13th and Aparri again on the 14th. The focus of the attack was then moved south, hitting the Manila area on the 15th. On 17 October, ENTERPRISE was assigned the task of escorting damaged ships to Ulithi but she was recalled on 22 October because the Japanese fleet was on the move.

Virtually all of their remaining fleet units set out from Brunei, Lingga and the home islands in a last desperate attempt to disrupt the American advance. ENTERPRISE took part in the Battle of the Sibuyan Sea, her aircraft attacking and eventually sinking the mammouth battleship MUSASHI on 24 October. Four days later, TG 38.4 took over direct support for the landings at Leyte. On 30 October, her task force mates, FRANKLIN and BELLEAU WOOD, were both hit by Kamikazes and both seriously damaged. After a quick visit to Ulithi, TG 38.4, now composed of ENTERPRISE and SAN JACINTO, attacked Japanese reinforcements enroute to Leyte on 11 November and then hit targets on Luzon on 13 and 14 November. ENTERPRISE retired to Ulithi on 23 November 1944.

At Ulithi, ENTERPRISE detached her air group and embarked a new one, this one specializing in night operations. On 30 December 1944, after working up the new air group. ENTERPRISE left Ulithi, along with the light carrier INDEPENDENCE and formed into TG 38.5, which was assigned to night combat duty during the forthcoming invasion of Luzon. Night operations were to be her specialty for the remainder of her career in the Pacific. On 10 January 1945, TF 5 (once again renamed) entered the South China

ENTERPRISE was hit by a single bomb on 20 March 1945, during raids on the Inland Sea. As the fast carrier task forces drew closer to Japan, the intensity of the defense, both conventional and kamikaze, grew. Although the damage was minor, ENTERPRISE was hit again in May and finally driven out of the war. (NARA)

Sea. ENTERPRISE launched a night attack on Cam Ranh Bay on 12 January and followed with attacks on Formosa and Fukien (now Fujian) Province of China on the 15th, Hong Kong on the 16th, Formosa again on the 21st and Okinawa on the 22nd, before returning to Ulithi on 25 January.

SARATOGA arrived back from her long refit at this time; like ENTERPRISE, she was also trained and equipped for night operations. Logically, the two old aircraft carriers were therefore joined together in TG 58.5, leaving Ulithi on 10 February. They raided the Tokyo area on 16 February, hit Yokohoma on the next day and then were detached from TF 58 to provide direct support for the landings of Iwo Jima. There, on 21 February, SARATOGA was hit by kamikazes and again knocked out of the war.

ENTERPRISE continued in action without SARATOGA, hitting Tokyo again on 25 and 26 February and Okinawa on 1 March. On 14 March, ENTERPRISE again sortied from Ulithi, now part of TG 58.2 with FRANKLIN. On 18 March, while attacking Kyushu, ENTERPRISE was slightly damaged by kamikazes. On the next day, FRANKLIN was hit by Japanese bombers and again severely damaged. ENTERPRISE was also hit, but the damage was minor. On 29 March, ENTERPRISE was assigned to TG 58.4, along with the new YORKTOWN, INTREPID and LANGLEY, with the task of continuing the aerial assault on Okinawa in preparation for the upcoming invasion. She was hit by kamikazes again on 11 April, this time seriously enough to require repairs at Ulithi. She was back off Okinawa again on 3 May, as part of TG 58.4. When the rest of that group retired on Ulithi on 10 May, ENTERPRISE transferred to TG 58.1, joining the new HORNET, BENNINGTON, RANDOLPH, BELLEAU WOOD and SAN JACINTO. The next day BUNKER HILL was seriously damaged by kamikazes, causing ADM Mitscher, now in charge of TF 58, to transfer his flag to ENTERPRISE. On the 12th and 13th, the entire task force raided the kamikaze airfields on Kyushu, trying to suppress these increasingly damaging attacks. On 14 May, having tempted fate perhaps once too often, ENTERPRISE was again hit by kamikazes, this time seriously. The damage was severe enough to send her back to the West Coast for repairs.

Neither ENTERPRISE nor SARATOGA saw further combat. SARATOGA completed her repairs during the Summer of 1945. She had been rebuilt with her aft elevator deleted, since she was obviously no longer needed as a combat aircraft carrier. The aft part of her hangar deck was divided into numerous classrooms, allowing her be used as a training aircraft carrier. The hugh amount of compartmented space in her hangar bay made her ideal as a transport for returning troops back to the U.S. as part of Operation

USS ENTERPRISE steams at high speed with a full deckload of aircraft. It was normal practice for U.S. carriers to carry their air wing on deck, using the hangar deck strictly for maintenance rather than storage. (NARA)

MAGIC CARPET. She was deleted from the active list soon thereafter, being consigned as a target ship for the atomic bomb tests conducted at Bikini Atoll. She proved to be a tough old lady to the end, surviving the Able test on 1 July 1946 with very little damage, but she sank as a result of damage inflicted during the Baker test on 25 July 1946.

ENTERPRISE fared only marginally better. She was ready for action again in July 1945, but was used solely for transport duties between the West Coast and Pearl Harbor. In October of 1945, she transferred to the Atlantic Fleet and was used extensively in the MAGIC CARPET between Europe and the East Coast. She remained in the Atlantic until 17 February 1947, when she was withdrawn from service and placed in reserve. She remained in mothballs until she was finally stricken from the Navy List on 2 October 1956. Attempts were made to buy her from the Navy and set her up as a memorial to the sailors and airmen who held the line in the dark early days of the war. She would have been the most fitting of memorials, but insufficient funds were collected and she was sold for scrap in 1958.

SARATOGA was similarly driven from the war by a Japanese air attack. Hit forward by multiple kamikazes, she was not seriously damaged, but was rendered incapable of operating aircraft. As a result, she was sent back to the West Coast for repairs. (NARA)

Other World War Two US Warships

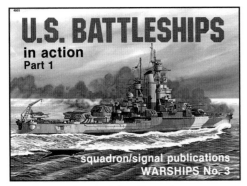

4003 US Battleships Part 1

4004 US Battleships Part 2

4008 Fletcher DDs

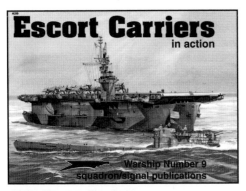

4009 Escort Carriers

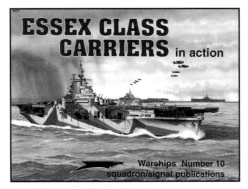

4010 Essex Class Carriers

4011 Destroyer Escorts

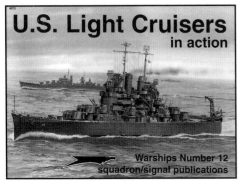

4012 US Light Cruisers

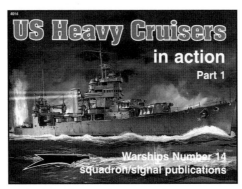

4014 US Heavy Cruisers Part 1

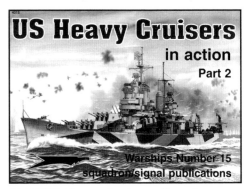

4015 US Heavy Cruisers Part 2

from squadron/signal publications